Y0-BVO-148

NEW DIRECTIONS FOR CHILD DEVELOPMENT

William Damon, *Brown University*
EDITOR-IN-CHIEF

Beliefs About Parenting: Origins and Developmental Implications

Judith G. Smetana
University of Rochester

EDITOR

Number 66, Winter 1994

JOSSEY-BASS PUBLISHERS
San Francisco

BELIEFS ABOUT PARENTING: ORIGINS AND DEVELOPMENTAL IMPLICATIONS
Judith G. Smetana (ed.)
New Directions for Child Development, no. 66
William Damon, Editor-in-Chief

Microfilm copies of issues and articles are available in 16mm and 35mm, as well as microfiche in 105mm, through University Microfilms Inc., 300 North Zeeb Road, Ann Arbor, Michigan 48106-1346.

LC 85-644581   ISSN 0195-2269   ISBN 0-7879-9984-9

NEW DIRECTIONS FOR CHILD DEVELOPMENT is part of The Jossey-Bass Education Series and is published quarterly by Jossey-Bass Inc., Publishers, 350 Sansome Street, San Francisco, California 94104-1342 (publication number USPS 494-090). Second-class postage paid at San Francisco, California, and at additional mailing offices. POSTMASTER: Send address changes to Jossey-Bass Inc., Publishers, 350 Sansome Street, San Francisco, California 94104-1342.

EDITORIAL CORRESPONDENCE should be sent to the Editor-in-Chief, William Damon, Department of Education, Box 1938, Brown University, Providence, Rhode Island 02912.

Cover photograph by Wernher Krutein/PHOTOVAULT © 1990.

Manufactured in the United States of America. Nearly all Jossey-Bass books, jackets, and periodicals are printed on recycled paper that contains at least 50 percent recycled waste, including 10 percent postconsumer waste. Many of our materials are also printed with vegetable-based inks; during the printing process these inks emit fewer volatile organic compounds (VOCs) than petroleum-based inks. VOCs contribute to the formation of smog.

CONTENTS

EDITOR'S NOTES

The exclusive interest among developmental psychologists in the influence of overt parenting practices and behaviors on child development has given way, in recent years, to a broader interest in the experience of parenting. After nearly a half century of research, developmental psychologists have discovered that parents, like their developing offspring, are cognizing individuals with goals, plans, ideas, motivations, intentions, and interests. Many factors, including the cognitive revolution in child development, the recognition that children may have reciprocal influences on parents (Bell, 1979), and the increasing interest in naive psychology, have contributed to this interest in parents' thinking about parenting (Goodnow and Collins, 1990). Although initially investigating parents' views primarily to improve the prediction of child outcomes, researchers more recently have become interested in parents' beliefs, values, and goals as a topic worthy of study in its own right.

Research on parents' beliefs (variously referred to as beliefs, ideas, or representations) has blossomed. As is often the case with new areas of investigation, research on parental beliefs has proceeded in many different directions, sometimes without unifying themes, clearly focused questions, or obvious directions. A brief perusal of the literature suggests that all of the traditional topics of child development have become fertile ground for examination from the perspective of parents' beliefs (see Goodnow, 1988; Goodnow and Collins, 1990; Holden and Edwards, 1989; Miller, 1986; Ashmore and Brodzinsky, 1986; Sigel, 1985; Sigel, McGillicuddy-DeLisi, and Goodnow, 1992). Thus, for instance, research on children's cognitive development has led to research on parents' ideas about children's cognitive development (Miller, 1986); research on parents' child rearing orientations has led to research on parents' attitudes about child rearing (Holden and Edwards, 1989), and research on the family has given way to research on parents' thinking about the family (Ashmore and Brodzinsky, 1986). Given the burgeoning interest in parental beliefs, it is time to reflect on the status of the field and to consider the available knowledge, conceptual frameworks, and questions for future research. This volume, *Parenting Beliefs: Origins and Developmental Implications*, brings together researchers from several different paradigms who have been at the forefront of this research. In these chapters, these researchers reflect on current knowledge, discuss new paradigms, and suggest new directions for research.

The first three chapters of the volume all focus on determinants of parenting beliefs. For instance, in Chapter One, Grusec, Hastings, and Mammone examine parents' attributions from the perspective of attachment theory. A great deal of recent research has begun to address the relevance of internal working models, as conceptualized within attachment theory (Main, Kaplan, and Cassidy, 1985), for adolescent and adult relationships and behavior. However, there have been few attempts to consider how internal working models influence parents' beliefs and behaviors. By making these important new connections, Grusec, Hastings, and Mammone suggest an important new way of conceptualizing and assessing the causes of parental behavior.

Typological models have dominated research on parental child rearing orientations. The chapters by me and by Youniss raise new questions about these approaches that could lead to significant revisions in how research on child rearing styles is conducted. In Chapter Two, I suggest that models of parenting style, such as Baumrind's (1978, 1988) popular model, are insensitive to variations in parenting that may be due to the characteristics of the different situations in which parenting is expressed. Thus, Baumrind argued for greater specificity in defining parenting orientations, both in terms of considering different domains of parental authority as well as in terms of distinguishing among different aspects of parenting orientations, such as parenting practices and parenting beliefs.

In Chapter Three, Youniss also notes the insensitivity of traditional models of parenting to contextual variations, but his discussion focuses on cultural and subcultural variation. He suggests that parenting beliefs are influenced by the broader societal context and proposes that parenting needs to be studied in this context. He illustrates this point, in a particularly timely way, by considering studies of parental beliefs among immigrant families, who must make transitions across different cultural contexts.

The next three chapters address the nature and consequences of parental beliefs. There has been a great deal of recent research on discrepancies between parents' and children's views of the family (for example, see Paikoff, 1991). In Chapter Four, Goodnow critically examines the meaning of such discrepancies. The overriding assumption of past research is that they indicate failures, dysfunction, or negative aspects of family functioning. Goodnow questions, in a novel way, what level and types of disagreements should be tolerated, or even celebrated, in families. Thus, her chapter is both a thoughtful and needed antidote to current research as well as a call for further research on this aspect of parental beliefs.

In Chapter Five, Collins and Luebker focus on parents' expectancies for their adolescents' behavior. The central thesis of their chapter is that violations of parents' expectancies, which are more likely during periods of rapid developmental change, provoke realignments in parent-adolescent relationships. To test this hypothesis, they describe a systematic program of research exploring the nature of parental expectancies, the extent of expectancy violations during adolescence, and the consequences of these violations for adolescent development. This research addresses a central question in developmental psychology: how changes in relationships maintain continuity of functioning.

Finally, in Chapter Six, Nucci draws on research indicating that children develop conceptions of personal issues and takes this research in an important new direction. He focuses on mothers' beliefs about what ought to be personal and up to their children to decide (rather than focusing on conceptual development in children). Through observational studies of mothers and children and interview studies with mothers, he demonstrates how personal concepts are constructed, negotiated, and elaborated in social interaction in cultural contexts.

Although the chapters in this volume represent diverse research approaches and address different research questions, there are several continuities in themes. First, research on parental beliefs has proceeded within many different theoretical paradigms. The chapters here characterize the plurality of theoretical voices that have addressed the topic of parental beliefs, but they also represent active attempts to synthesize different theoretical perspectives. Grusec, Hastings, and Mammone demonstrate the relevance of considering parents' internal working models, as specified within attachment theory, to parents' causal attributions. I argue for the integration of typological models of parenting, as exemplified by Baumrind's model of parenting styles, with normative developmental research on domain-differentiated conceptions of parental authority. Youniss integrates traditional developmental approaches to child rearing with the insights of sociological theories. The questions raised in Goodnow's chapter arise from the links she draws between studies of "classic" cognition and newer studies examining cultural models (D'Andrade and Strauss, 1992). Collins and Luebker's social-cognitive approach to parental expectancies is informed by social-psychological theories of close relationships (Kelley and others, 1983). And Nucci presents a structural-developmental model of social cognition but considers how development varies in cultural contexts. Thus, each of these chapters points to new ways of conceptualizing parental beliefs that stretch the boundaries of traditional theoretical views.

Second, many of these chapters focus attention on the context in which parental beliefs emerge and are expressed. By examining lower- and middle-class parents' beliefs about the personal domain of children in the United States and in two regions of Brazil, Nucci calls attention to how cultural beliefs are negotiated and constructed within different cultures. Rather than take a top-down approach, however, where cultures are seen to impose knowledge on individuals, Nucci argues that instances of conflict and child resistance suggest that individuals construct social knowledge within different cultural frames. Cultural variation is the central theme of Youniss's chapter. Youniss argues that researchers have failed to take cultural knowledge and beliefs into account and that parental beliefs are inseparable from the cultural context in which they arise. Goodnow also argues for the need to interpret discrepancies between parents' and children's beliefs in terms of cultural messages about child rearing. Collins and Luebker, Grusec, Hastings, and Mammone, and I are also sensitive to contextual issues, considering how parental beliefs may differ in different ethnic and socioeconomic contexts and in the context of different child rearing orientations.

Finally, previous research on parental beliefs has focused primarily on parents of young children. The issues raised by and the insights gained from each of these chapters demonstrate the relevance and importance of considering parental beliefs across a wide age range of children and adolescents. These chapters represent significant advances in understanding parental beliefs and their role in child and adolescent development.

Judith G. Smetana
Editor

References

Ashmore, R. D., and Brodzinsky, D. M. (eds.). *Thinking About Family: Views of Parents and Children.* Hillsdale, N.J.: Erlbaum, 1986.

Baumrind, D. "Parental Disciplinary Patterns and Social Competence in Children." *Youth and Society,* 1978, *9* (2), 239–276.

Baumrind, D. "Rearing Competent Children." In W. Damon (ed.), *Child Development Today and Tomorrow.* San Francisco: Jossey-Bass, 1988.

Bell, R. Q. "Parent, Child, and Reciprocal Influences." *American Psychologist,* 1979, *34,* 821–826.

D'Andrade, R. G., and Strauss, C. *Human Motives and Cultural Models.* New York: Cambridge University Press, 1992.

Goodnow, J. J. "Parents' Ideas, Actions, and Feelings: Models and Methods from Developmental and Social Psychology." *Child Development,* 1988, *59* (2), 286–320.

Goodnow, J. J., and Collins, W. A. *Development According to Parents: The Nature, Sources, and Consequences of Parents' Ideas.* Hillsdale, N.J.: Erlbaum, 1990.

Holden, G. W., and Edwards, L. A. "Parental Attitudes Towards Child Rearing: Instruments, Issues, and Implications." *Psychological Bulletin,* 1989, *106* (1), 29–58.

Kelley, H. H., Berscheid, E., Christensen, A., Harvey, J. H., Huston, T. L., Levinger, G., McClintock, E., Peplau, L. A., and Peterson, D. R. *Close Relationships.* New York: Freeman, 1983.

Main, M., Kaplan, N., and Cassidy, J. "Security in Infancy, Childhood, and Adulthood: A Move to the Level of Representation." In I. Bretherton and E. Waters (eds.), *Growing Points of Attachment: Theory and Research.* Monographs of the Society for Research in Child Development, vol. 50, nos. 1–2 (serial no. 209). Chicago: University of Chicago Press, 1985.

Miller, S. A. "Parents' Beliefs About Their Children's Cognitive Abilities." *Developmental Psychology,* 1986, *22* (2), 276–284.

Paikoff, R. L. (ed.). *Shared Views in the Family During Adolescence.* New Directions for Child Development, no. 51. San Francisco: Jossey-Bass, 1991.

Sigel, I. E. (ed.). *Parental Belief Systems: The Psychological Consequences for Children.* Hillsdale, N.J.: Erlbaum, 1985.

Sigel, I. E., McGillicuddy-DeLisi, A. V., and Goodnow, J. J. (eds.). *Parental Belief Systems: The Psychological Consequences for Children.* (2nd ed.) Hillsdale, N.J.: Erlbaum, 1992.

JUDITH G. SMETANA *is professor of education, psychology, and pediatrics at the University of Rochester, Rochester, New York.*

A primary source of parents' feelings of self-efficacy with respect to child rearing, as well as their explanations for their children's misdeeds, is the mental representations of relationships they have developed.

Parenting Cognitions and Relationship Schemas

Joan E. Grusec, Paul Hastings, Norma Mammone

Studies of parenting cognitions have been diverse in nature. In summarizing this diversity, Goodnow and Collins (1990) listed a number of domains of parenting beliefs that they characterized as having to do with directions of development and with conditions of development. Among the former are parents' goals, ideas about starting points such as expectations of what children may be like, and beliefs about how children develop. With respect to the latter, Goodnow and Collins cited ideas about the relative contributions of internal and external events, the influence and responsibility of parents, and the methods that parents might use to achieve various goals.

Researchers who have studied this array of parenting cognitions have focused mostly on the effects of these cognitions on parenting behavior and child outcomes (for example, Sigel, McGillicuddy-DeLisi, and Goodnow, 1992). In our recent work, we addressed another question having to do with parenting cognitions, namely, the nature of their origins. We hypothesized that parenting cognitions are affected by the particular cultural context in which parents find themselves as well as by the specific experiences they have had with their own children. Our primary focus, however, is on the proposal that the childhood experiences parents have with their own caretakers are a major source of at least some of these cognitions, and that schemas or beliefs about relationships that develop as a result of those early experiences form the basis of specific thoughts about parenting.

The research described in this chapter focused on two specific sets of parenting cognitions: parents' feelings of self-efficacy and their attributions concerning their children's behavior. Parenting self-efficacy refers to parents' expectations about their ability to effectively influence their children's behav-

5

ior. According to Bandura (1977), for example, parents who believe they do not have the ability to parent successfully do not put their knowledge of parenting into action, become preoccupied with themselves, are emotionally aroused, and do not persist at the task of parenting. Bugental (for example, Bugental and Shennum, 1984; Bugental, 1991) focused on how much power parents believe themselves to have in situations of conflict with their children relative to the power they attribute to their children. She demonstrated that mothers who are low in relative perceived power experience negative affect, have problem-focused thoughts, and engage in power-assertive or punitive child rearing. Attributions about children's behavior refer to the degree to which parents believe that their children's behavior was intentional and foreseen, as well as free from external control. To the extent that this is the case, parents are assumed to assign blame and responsibility to their children in the cases of misdeeds and to attribute their behavior to dispositional characteristics rather than external situational constraints and forces. Dix and his colleagues (for example, Dix and Grusec, 1985; Dix, Ruble, and Zambarano, 1989) found the expected relations among different kinds of attributions. As well, they demonstrated that these thoughts or attributions are associated with parental anger and punitive reactions.

Sources of Parenting Cognitions

How might cognitions about self-efficacy and attributions for children's behavior arise? We discuss in turn each of three possible sources: the culture in which individuals find themselves, experiences parents have with their own children, and experiences parents have had interacting with their own parents. Our argument is that although culture and experiences with children can give rise to a number of different kinds of parenting cognitions, those having to do with self-efficacy and attributions for children's behavior may be particularly likely to originate in childhood experiences.

Sources of Parenting Cognitions in the Culture. Cultures and communities deliver many messages about parenting. Bronfenbrenner (for example, 1977) pointed to the importance of the macrosystem or the broader community in the communication of normative cultural standards about child rearing through advice from relatives and experts, or through the witnessing of interactions within families other than one's own. Goodnow (1985) refined the realm of the possible influence of culture by suggesting that one's culture is the primary source of information about the facts of child rearing, that is, what children are like at various ages, what parenting techniques work, and what goals parents should value. Indeed, researchers have identified cultural differences in parents' expected developmental timetables, and some have extended this investigation to what parents think guides or influences those changes (for example, Keller, Miranda, and Gauda, 1984; Ninio, 1979; Sameroff and Feil, 1985). As well, cultural variations in the child rearing values held by parents have been examined. Middle-class, Caucasian North American parents, for example, have been described as placing greater emphasis on the fostering of autonomy and independence in their children than do members of many other cultural groups, such as those who place greater value on family or community identification and affiliation (Conroy, Hess, Szuma, and Kashiwagi, 1980; Gfellner, 1990; Goodnow and Collins, 1990; Kelley and Tseng, 1992).

More specific kinds of cognitions, however, may not be equally amenable to cultural influences. The failure of Moss and Jones (1977) to find differences between middle-class and lower-class mothers in their child rearing attributions suggests that these particular cognitions might be more intimately tied to something other than the messages of their cultural or socioeconomic groups. Moreover, although more general belief systems such as those having to do with developmental timetables, methods of change, and values may be affected by culture, there is also a great deal of individual variation within groups for these systems. Goodnow (1985) argued that parents are not passive recipients of their culture's messages but that they filter them. Accordingly, parents seek out one another to discuss child rearing values, and the social networks they form serve to build their beliefs (Cohen, 1981) and to reinforce those cognitions that they see as fitting with their community's expectations (Crnic and others, 1983; Kelley, Power, and Wimbush, 1992). If there are several cultural values, then, individuals could selectively attend to the societal messages appearing to match their own beliefs. This argument has been advanced to explain how abusive parents may see their behavior as not falling outside the norms of their society: Despite the broad cultural values of raising children to be autonomous, competent, and independent, North American culture also views children as possessions of their parents, as accepting of corporal punishment, and as generally quite violent (Belsky, 1980; Cicchetti and Rizley, 1981). Thus, there are ample models in the culture that could support maltreating parents' child rearing beliefs.

A second possible explanation for individual variation in beliefs is that experience with cultural standards at odds with one's own practices might drive a parent to decrease contact with contradictory opinions, rather than to conform. Studies of child maltreatment support this proposal. Abusive families are more socially isolated than nonabusive families (Kaufman and Zigler, 1989), and abusive parents place less value on their children's openness to experiences and on their autonomy than do nonabusive parents (Trickett and Susman, 1988). It seems that abusive parents may attempt to minimize both their own and their children's exposure to moderating influences from the community.

It would be surprising if such a pervasive feature of life as the cultural context did not have an impact on some aspects of parent cognitions. However, this is only one source of influence, and possibly not the most important, at least for more specific parenting cognitions such as self-efficacy and attributions. We turn, then, to a second candidate for influence, parents' experiences raising their children.

Sources of Parenting Cognitions in Experiences with Children. It seems highly plausible that an important determinant of parental belief systems is the specific child rearing experiences of parents. Supporting evidence for this proposition is far from strong, however. This is in part because some parenting cognitions may be more subject to influence from the experience of raising children than are others. Just as it has been argued that culture may have more impact on global than specific beliefs, the reverse argument has been made in the case of child rearing experiences. Murphy (1992), for example, suggested that more global beliefs, that is, parents' expectations or naive theories about how and when children develop different abilities or traits, as well as parents' goals, may be particularly resilient to change as they are not tied to specific interactions or contexts of child rearing. For example, women of different cultural backgrounds expect many developmental milestones to occur at different times (Hess and others, 1980; Ninio, 1979), and they do not change these beliefs even after they have raised a child. Similarly, McGillicuddy-DeLisi (1982) reported that parents' beliefs about what causes children to learn and develop are not related to the amount of experience they have as parents. Boggiano and others (1987) demonstrated how firmly held beliefs about how to influence children's development (for example, that rewarding children for good grades is a good way to encourage intrinsic motivation for doing well at school) are highly resistant to disconfirming evidence from outside the family (that is, reports of the results of psychological studies).

Goodnow (1985) argued that more specific beliefs such as parents' thoughts concerning their own competence and effectiveness might be more susceptible to feedback from parent-child encounters. If these beliefs are affected by experience with a parent's own child, for example, then the temperament of that child should be predictive of parenting efficacy. The evidence is mixed, however. In some cases infant temperament and low parenting efficacy are related (Teti and Gelfand, 1991), while in others they are not (Donovan, Leavitt, and Walsh, 1990). Negative attitudes and attributions about children that exist in parents before their children are born are predictive of problematic relationships postnatally (Moss and Jones, 1977), a finding that suggests such attributions predate experience with children. Abusive parents have low self-efficacy even before they have accumulated much experience as parents (Mash and Johnston, 1990) and are biased toward making negative attributions for their children's behavior (Larrance and Twentyman, 1983); moreover, they have biased perceptions of their children even when those children are not behaving differently from nonabused children (Mash and Johnston, 1982). On the other hand, Mash and Johnston (1983) reported that parents of children with attention deficit hyperactivity disorder (ADHD) had lower parenting efficacy than parents of nonproblem children, and that those who had been parents of children with ADHD for longer had lower self-efficacy than did those with younger children. In contrast, the self-efficacy of parents of nonproblem children was positively correlated with their children's age. When their children's hyperactivity was compounded with extreme defiance, parents were especially likely to develop more negative and dispositional attributions for the disruptive behavior of children with ADHD, such as believing that their children were deliberately malicious and holding them responsible for any serious trouble they got into (Barkley, Anastopoulos, Guevremont, and Fletcher, 1992). From these studies, we suggest that when faced repeatedly with evidence that they are unable to moderate the behavior of exceptionally uncontrollable children, parents are in danger of developing the undesirable cognitions of low self-efficacy and negatively biased attributions for their children's behavior.

Clearly, at least some experiences as a parent can influence feelings of self-efficacy and attributions for children's misdeeds. This conclusion seems more pronounced in studies involving parents of problem children, however. What is striking is the absence of strong effects in the case of normally functioning families. Thus, we turn to an alternative source for the formulation of these particular parental belief systems. In the next section, we argue that parents' own socialization experiences are a powerful source of beliefs about parenting, and we present data showing that the mental representations of relationships that parents derive from their own experiences as children have a strong bearing on their parenting cognitions.

Sources of Parenting Cognitions in Relationship Schemas. Our argument is that parenting cognitions or belief systems can be seen as part of the internal representations of relationships that individuals bring with them to any interaction with others, including, but not limited to, their own children. Accordingly, the thoughts parents have when they are dealing with children should be similar in kind to the thoughts they have in any close social interaction, whether it involves spouses, friends, or their own parents. The suggestion is that individuals possess cognitive structures that represent regularities in their patterns of interpersonal relating. These "cognitive maps" that "help [individuals] to navigate their social world" (Baldwin, 1992, p. 462) include images of the self and of others, along with a script for an expected manner of interaction. The idea that cognitive maps may be guiding behavior in the domain of parenting cognitions also has been suggested by Bugental (for example, Bugental, 1991; Bugental and others, 1993), who referred in her work to a schema or cognitive construction of relative power in relationships that is chronically accessible, operates below the level of conscious awareness, and sensitizes individuals to specific events in the environment. Our proposal is that, for relationships in general, people have interpersonal or relationship schemas that include feelings of relative control in social interactions as well as attributions for the behavior of others. Parenting cognitions are simply these beliefs as they are manifested in a particular kind of social relationship, namely, child rearing. We suggest that these constructions of relationships determine the individual's cognitive, affective, and behavioral reaction to a social situation. One can understand the development of parenting cognitions, then, by understanding the development of general cognitions or beliefs having to do with oneself in relation to others.

Development of Relationship Schemas. How, then, do these relationship schemas arise? The most thorough investigation and detailed description currently available of the development of thoughts or ideas about relationships come from attachment theory. According to Bowlby (1973), early experiences with caregivers provide the child with material for the construction of mental working models of the world that include both the self and significant others. The models are described as "working" because individuals use them to generate interpretations of present events as well as to evaluate alternative possible future actions. Thus, the models provide rules that direct social behavior as well as determine the ways in which social experiences are appraised. They are described as "models" because they are constructed throughout the course of development, initially being simple but becoming increasingly complex. Working models, once they are formulated, tend to be resistant to dramatic change both because they usually operate outside conscious awareness and because new information is assimilated into existing models (Bowlby, 1980).

Early in the course of development the self and significant others are closely intertwined in the model, so that internal working models are models of a relationship. Over time, however, models of the self and of the other become distinct. Nevertheless, neither the self nor the other can ever be understood independently, but only in relationship to each other. Thus, a child who is rejected comes to see both the caretaker as rejecting and the self as worthy of rejection (Main, Kaplan, and Cassidy, 1985). Sroufe and Fleason (1985) went further to suggest that individuals internalize both sides of a relationship, so that they can exhibit either the behavior of the self or the behavior of the other, depending on the context. For example, the rejected child grows up to be an adult who can be rejecting when the situation is appropriate or the object of rejection when the situation is appropriate. In this way attachment theory points to two possible outcomes of early experiences, identification with or reproduction of the behavior of a caretaker as well as behavior in keeping with self-perceptions developed as a function of experience with and feedback from that caretaker.

Attachment theory identifies three primary models of relationships (Ainsworth, Blehar, Waters, and Wall, 1978). Sensitive and responsive parents produce children who are securely attached and who know that their emotional needs will be met. Rejecting parents create insecure avoidantly attached children who learn not to display either distress or anger. Inconsistently responsive and sensitive parents have children who are anxiously resistant in their attachment behavior, and who display heightened expressions of distress in an attempt to ensure parental responsiveness and anger in reaction to lack of parental responsiveness. These three prototypes of relationships, learned early in life, are alleged to direct behavior throughout the life span. They determine, as an example, the degree to which individuals feel efficacious in social situations. Two other attachment types have also been identified, one a mixture of avoidant and resistant features and the other disorganized (see Bretherton, 1992), but less is known about their antecedents and outcomes.

There is an emphasis in attachment theory on very early experiences with caretakers, with the argument that early models are resistant to change for the reasons noted above. Nevertheless, we do know that working models of relationships can alter in response to changing environmental conditions (Egeland, Jacobvitz, and Sroufe, 1988). It is not unreasonable to suggest, then, that models of relationships continue to be modified (or strengthened) throughout the course of socialization. Recently, Grusec and Mammone (in press) argued, for example, that perceptions of the nature of social relationships can be learned during the discipline interaction. They suggest that authoritarian parents, who demand obedience and are unresponsive to the desires of the child (Baumrind, 1991), teach their children that in situations of conflict the self has little control over outcomes while the other has substantial control. Because authoritarian parents are more inclined to make dispositional attributions for their children's misdeeds (Dix, Ruble, and Zambarano, 1989), Grusec and Mammone suggested that authoritarian parents also teach their children, through modeling, that the behavior of others is internally rather than situationally driven. Thus, we suggest that models of relationships continue to be modified as a result of child rearing experiences having to do not only with attachment but with control issues as well.

Assessing Mental Representations of Relationships. Models of relationships in infancy have been assessed using Ainsworth's Strange Situation. In recent years investigators have turned their attention to assessment during adolescence and adulthood. One method of assessment is that developed by Main and Goldwyn (1991). In Main and Goldwyn's Adult Attachment Interview (AAI), adolescents and adults are asked a variety of questions about childhood attachment experiences. From the way they respond to these questions, it is possible to assess their *current state of mind* with respect to early attachment experiences. It must be stressed that actual childhood experiences, the presumed nature of previous attachments, or presumed previous states of mind are not what are assessed. What is measured is the adult's present state of mind with respect to these experiences and the nature of his or her discourse about them. It is this present state of mind that is considered relevant for the conceptualization and direction of present social behavior.

Three major patterns of organization have been identified that conceptually parallel infant patterns of attachment. Adults classified as secure-autonomous appear to value attachment but are able to be objective in evaluating their own particular experiences. Actual experience may be inferred to have been either positive or negative, but the state of mind with respect to this experience is coherent, open, and objective. Adults classified as dismissive of attachment attempt to limit the influence of attachment relationships in their thinking, feeling, and behavior, while making an implicit claim to strength, normality, and independence. Finally, individuals classified as preoccupied with early attachments or past experiences seem confused, unobjective, and mentally entangled in their descriptions, being either passive and vague, fearful and overwhelmed, or angry, conflicted, and unconvincingly analytical. The

AAI also identifies individuals who are unresolved with respect to the loss of an attachment figure or some other traumatic event. Individuals given primary assignment to this category are also categorized in terms of whether they are secure-autonomous, dismissive, or preoccupied.

The AAI has considerable validity as a measure of the individual's mental representation of attachment relationships. Thus, there is a high degree of concordance between a mother's current attachment classification and that of her infant (van IJzendoorn, 1992), an indication that contemporary ways of thinking about relationships determine parenting behavior. The fact that this concordance is high even when maternal attachment is measured prior to the infant's birth (Fonagy, Steele, and Steele, 1991) indicates that the mother's quality of discourse on the AAI is not the result of the nature of the relationship she has formed with her infant. Rather, it appears that a mother's way of viewing relationships is an important determinant of how she reacts to her own child and her developing relationship with that child. Also, maternal attachment categories have been reported to be related to mothers' interactions with their preschoolers in teaching situations and in situations that involve separation and reunion (Crowell and Feldman, 1988, 1991). Finally, Bakersman-Kranenburg and van IJzendoorn (1993) found high test-retest reliability for the AAI over a two-month period. They also reported that AAI classifications are independent of verbal and performance intelligence, social desirability, and memory for childhood events not related to attachment issues.

Relationship Schemas and Parenting Cognitions. Descriptions of the thinking and behavior of secure, dismissive, and preoccupied individuals provide a starting point for our argument about the specific way in which mental representations of relationships might determine cognitions. These descriptions are based on the work of Main and Goldwyn (1991) and Crowell and Feldman (1988). Secure individuals are coherent, open, and objective in their dealings with other individuals and presumably are less inclined toward biased or threatening, or both, interpretations of ambiguous events. In their specific interactions with children they are emotionally supportive, clear, and consistent in their attempts at socialization, as well as responsive, sensitive, and self-confident. When considering their relationships with their own parents, they acknowledge mutual responsibility for outcomes. In contrast, dismissive adults, who frequently report the experience of childhood rejection, negate the importance of attachment relationships and stress their own independence and strength. In their interactions with their children they have a task-focused style characterized by coolness and remoteness and they are not very emotionally supportive or helpful. They see their parents as having had little impact or effect on them. In sharp contrast to dismissive ways of thinking and behaving are the thoughts and behaviors of preoccupied adults. In their interactions with their children they are inconsistent and often confusing. At times they are warm and gentle, while at other times they appear coercive, puzzled, or angry. They are deeply enmeshed in relationships in such a way that differentiation between themselves and others becomes difficult. With respect to their relationships with their own parents, they assign blame for difficulties solely to their parents and appear unable to understand their own role in such difficulties.

These descriptions led us to make the following predictions about relations between attachment style and parenting cognitions. Dismissive parents will go to great lengths to maintain an image of themselves as strong, normal, and independent, and they will not allow a child's misbehavior to threaten this image. Thus, we hypothesized that they attribute low control over failure to themselves and high control to their child, as well as high degrees of intentionality to that child. Given their apparent (surface) high degree of self-confidence, they also express few negative thoughts about their parenting abilities. In contrast, we predicted that preoccupied parents, always determined to place responsibility on the parent, will attribute high control to themselves. Also, in accord with their views on responsibility in the child rearing situation, they will not attribute control over bad behavior, or intentionality, to the child. Because of their inclination to be preoccupied with difficulties in relationships, we also predicted that preoccupied individuals will have more negative thoughts in unsuccessful child rearing situations.

Mental Representations, Self-Efficacy, Negative Ideation, and Attributions for Children's Behavior. Our research (Grusec, Adam, and Mammone, 1993), designed to test these hypotheses, involved the participation of seventy-four mothers and twenty fathers of children between the ages of four and seven years. Twenty-seven of the children had been exposed to some form of maltreatment, and sixty-seven came from a control group matched for family income and education.

To assess their mental representations of relationships, parents were administered the AAI. On the basis of the interview, they were assigned to one of the three main classifications of secure-autonomous, dismissive, and preoccupied. Individuals whose primary classification was unresolved were placed into their secondary category. Intercoder agreement for classifications was .87, based on number of agreements divided by the sum of number of agreements and number of disagreements. In the case of disagreement, a classification was made after discussion. Our coders had also achieved satisfactory agreement on an independent set of AAI transcripts coded by Mary Main. There were significant differences between maltreating and control parents in attachment status, with nine of thirteen dismissive individuals and seven of nine preoccupied individuals coming from the maltreating group. There was no difference between mothers and fathers in pattern of attachment classification.

To assess parenting self-efficacy, Bugental's Parent Attribution Test (Bugental and Shennum, 1984) was used. In this test parents are asked to assign importance to a variety of factors determining hypothesized unsuccessful outcomes in interactions with children. The test yields two causal factors: whether outcomes are attributed to the adult or the child and whether these outcomes are seen as controllable or uncontrollable. Examples of controllable outcomes include use of the wrong child rearing approach and how well one gets along with children in general (for the adult) and stubbornness and lack of effort made to take an interest in what was said or done (for the child). Examples of uncontrollable events include mood, fatigue, and the weather. On the basis of endorsement of these items, two scores are calculated, adult control over failure and child control over failure. The difference between these two scores yields a third measure, perceived control over failure.

The second set of parenting cognitions assessed was the negative thoughts parents reported having during difficult interactions with their children. Each parent was videotaped with his or her child in a playroom setting and asked to persuade the child to clean up at the end of a period of play. Later, the parent was shown a videotape of this segment of the interaction and asked to identify a time when things were not going well and he or she thought that the child was acting badly. The parents were then given a list of ten thoughts that parents sometimes have and asked to check off those items that had come to mind. Half the thoughts were negative, for example, "I can't take it much longer" and "I feel ineffective and helpless; nothing I do seems to work."

Attributions for children's behavior were obtained by having parents read a series of vignettes describing children's misdeeds and asking them to imagine that the child in each story was their own. Parents were then asked to rate on a 7-point scale their responses to a series of questions about the extent to which the child knew he or she had behaved badly, how much blame he or she deserved for the bad behavior, and whether the behavior was due to his or her personality or to the situation. Low scores indicated low knowledge, low blame, and attributions to the situation. Knowledge and blame scores were highly correlated and were combined to produce a score reflecting attributions of intentionality.

Parent Attribution Test scores, number of negative thoughts endorsed in response to the difficult time, and attributions for children's behavior are presented in Table 1.1 for each attachment group. Preoccupied parents perceived themselves as having significantly more control over failure than did either secure or dismissive parents. Dismissive parents rated their children's control over failure as higher than secure parents, who rated it, in turn, higher than preoccupied parents. Thus, our proposals about the nature of perceptions of control in child rearing were confirmed. When scores on child control over failure were subtracted from scores on adult control over failure to yield an overall measure of perceived control over failure, preoccupied parents saw themselves as having most control and dismissive parents saw themselves as having least control. In essence, as we suggested earlier, dismissive and preoccupied parents appeared to have taken over or identified with what they saw as their own parents' role. For dismissive individuals, this means being an adult who has little influence over an independent and self-sufficient child. In the case of preoccupied individuals, it means being an adult who has great influence over a child who is relatively powerless in comparison.

As we had predicted, it was the preoccupied parents who endorsed the most negative thoughts, presumably a reflection of their high degree of rumination over difficulties they experience. Dismissive individuals expressed few

Table 1.1. Scores on the Parent Attribution Test, Negative Thoughts During a Difficult Interaction with Child, and Attributions for Children's Behavior as a Function of Attachment Classification

	Attachment Classification		
Parenting Cognition	Secure	Dismissive	Preoccupied
Adult control over failure	4.26^a	4.15^a	4.94^b
Child control over failure	4.02^b	4.50^c	3.54^a
Perceived control over failure	$.24^b$	$-.35^a$	1.40^c
Negative thoughts	$.39^a$	$.87^a$	1.43^b
Attributions to intentionality	4.82^a	4.35^a	4.47^a
Attributions to personality	2.64^a	3.07^a	3.87^b

Note: High scores indicate high control over failure, high intentionality, and high attribution to personality. Different superscripts across each line indicate statistically significant differences between groups.

negative thoughts, presumably in keeping with their desire to present themselves as self-confident and assured.

Our predictions about child attributes were not supported (see Table 1.1). Attributions to intentionality did not distinguish among attachment categories. Attributions to personality did, however, but in a direction contrary to what we had hypothesized. Thus, preoccupied parents were more likely to attribute failure to the personalities of their children than were dismissive or secure parents. How might we explain these unexpected outcomes? Consider, first, the failure to find any relation between attachment category and attributions of knowledge and intentionality. Our argument is that some parenting cognitions have their basis in mental models of relationships, that is, in ideas about the self in relation to others. Decisions about children's knowledge or intentions do not, in fact, require a weighing of the nature of the relationship between the child and the parent. Causes of behavior reside in the child and do not involve a consideration of features of the child and the parent in relationship to each other in the same way as do decisions about self-efficacy. This may be why we did not find the predicted relation. And what of the finding that preoccupied parents were more likely to attribute failure to the personalities of their children? We suggest this outcome may reflect the difficulty that preoccupied individuals have differentiating between themselves and others by virtue of their general enmeshment in relationships. Although they believe they have control over negative outcomes in caregiving situations, they also ascribe problem behavior to enduring features of their children in order to alleviate any indications of their own failure.

Conclusion

The research described in this chapter demonstrated a relation between the mental representations of relationships that parents carry with them and at least some aspects of their parenting cognitions. Thus, individuals classified as dismissive saw themselves as having less power than their children in a diffi-cult child rearing situation. In keeping with a facade of strength and indepen-dence, they reported experiencing fewer negative thoughts when they found their interactions with their children were not going well. On the other hand, preoccupied individuals perceived that they had greater power than their chil-dren in difficult child rearing situations. At the same time, however, they expe-rienced many negative thoughts and attributed their lack of success to personality characteristics of their children. We have suggested that these fea-tures of parental thinking are generally consistent with the way individuals have of viewing themselves and others in relationships. Thus, we claim that an understanding of how parenting cognitions develop necessitates an under-standing of how relationship schemas develop, and that one place to look for the origins of parenting belief systems, therefore, is in childhood experiences with caretakers who are sensitive and accepting, or rejecting, or inconsistent in the way they respond to the needs of their offspring.

What are the next steps to be taken in understanding the origins of par-enting cognitions? One obvious direction has to do with links among rela-tionship schemas, parenting cognitions, and parenting affect and behavior. We know that attachment classification is related to some parenting cognitions. We know that parenting cognitions have an impact on emotions and, directly as well as indirectly (through their impact on emotion), on parenting behav-ior. We now must ask about relations between attachment classification and parental responses to children's misdeeds, and, if they exist, we must deter-mine whether they are indeed mediated by parenting cognitions. Such a demonstration would provide support for the argument that how parents react to their children's problematic behavior is determined by the early experiences they have had with their own parents, with these experiences giving rise to modes of thinking that determine affect and behavior. Indeed, our findings suggest that children of dismissive and preoccupied parents may be at some risk for maladaptive parenting, given their large representation in the group of maltreating parents we assessed.

A second direction in which research on the sources of parenting cogni-tions might proceed is toward assessing the relative impact of culture, parent-ing experience, and early experience with being parented on various cognitions having to do with the directions and conditions of development. Our research suggests that parenting self-efficacy may be more affected by early experience than are parents' beliefs about the intentionality of their children's behavior. We have presented the point of view that more general beliefs having to do with developmental timetables, methods of changing children's behavior, and values are more likely to be influenced by the culture in which one lives, whereas more specific beliefs about self-efficacy and negatively biased attribu-tions are more likely to be affected by specific experiences with one's own child. These hypotheses remain to be tested.

Obviously, much remains to be done with respect to identifying the ori-gins of parenting cognitions. The question of origin is important, however. Not only will knowledge of how different parenting cognitions are acquired expand our understanding of the determinants of the parenting process, but such knowledge will make it easier to modify parenting behavior that is less than optimal. In our society, there is increasing attention to and concern with the frequency of child maltreatment. Knowledge of the role of different parental belief systems in this maltreatment and of the different origins of these belief systems will be crucial in attempts to modify maltreatment as well as to prevent its occurrence in the first place.

References

Ainsworth, M.D.S., Blehar, M. C., Waters, E., and Wall, S. *Patterns of Attachment: A Psychological Study of the Strange Situation.* Hillsdale, N.J.: Erlbaum, 1978.

Bakersman-Kranenburg, M. J., and van IJzendoorn, M. H. "A Psychometric Study of the Adult Attachment Interview: Reliability and Discriminant Validity." *Developmental Psychology,* 1993, *29* (5), 870–879.

Baldwin, M. J. "Relational Schemas and the Processing of Social Information." *Psychological Review,* 1992, *112* (3), 461–484.

Bandura, A. "Self-Efficacy: Toward a Unifying Theory of Behavior Change." *Psychological Review,* 1977, *84* (2), 191–215.

Barkley, R. A., Anastopoulos, A. D., Guevremont, D. C., and Fletcher, K. E. "Adolescents with Attention Deficit Hyperactivity Disorder: Mother-Adolescent Interactions, Family Beliefs and Conflicts, and Maternal Psychopathology." *Journal of Abnormal Child Psychology,* 1992, *20* (3), 263–288.

Baumrind, D. "Effective Parenting During the Early Adolescent Transition." In P. A. Cowan and E. M. Hetherington (eds.), *Advances in Family Research.* Vol. 2. Hillsdale, N.J.: Erlbaum, 1991.

Belsky, J. "Child Maltreatment: An Ecological Integration." *American Psychologist,* 1980, *35* (8), 747–755.

Boggiano, A. K., Barret, M., Weiher, A. W., McClelland, G. H., and Lusk, C. M. "Use of the Maximum-Operant Principle to Motivate Children's Intrinsic Interest." *Journal of Personality and Social Psychology,* 1987, *53* (5), 866–879.

Bowlby, J. *Attachment and Loss.* Vol. 2: *Separation.* New York: Basic Books, 1973.

Bowlby, J. *Attachment and Loss.* Vol. 3: *Loss, Sadness, and Depression.* New York: Basic Books, 1980.

Bretherton, I. "The Origins of Attachment Theory: John Bowlby and Mary Ainsworth." *Developmental Psychology,* 1992, *28* (5), 759–775.

Bronfenbrenner, U. "Toward an Experimental Ecology of Human Development." *American Psychologist,* 1977, *52,* 513–531.

Bugental, D. B. "Affective and Cognitive Processes Within Threat-Oriented Family Systems." In I. E. Sigel, A. V. McGillicuddy-DeLisi, and J. J. Goodnow (eds.), *Parental Belief Systems: The Psychological Consequences for Children.* (2nd ed.) Hillsdale, N.J.: Erlbaum, 1991.

Bugental, D. B., Blue, J., Cortez, V., Fleck, K., Kopeikin, H., Lewis, J. C., and Lyon, J. "Social Cognitions as Organizers of Autonomic and Affective Responses to Social Challenge." *Journal of Personality and Social Psychology,* 1993, *64,* 94–103.

Bugental, D. B., and Shennum, W. A. *"Difficult" Children as Elicitors and Targets of Adult Communication Patterns: An Attributional-Behavioral Transactional Analysis.* Monographs of the Society for Research in Child Development, vol. 49, no. 1 (serial no. 205). Chicago: University of Chicago Press, 1984.

Cicchetti, D., and Rizley, R. "Developmental Perspectives on the Etiology, Intergenerational Transmission, and Sequalae of Child Maltreatment." *New Directions for Child Maltreatment,* 1981, *11* (1), 31–55.

Cohen, G. "Culture and Educational Achievement." *Harvard Educational Review,* 1981, *51* (2), 270–285.

Conroy, M., Hess, R. D., Szuma, H., and Kashiwagi, K. "Maternal Strategies for Regulating Children's Behavior: Japanese and American Families." *Journal of Cross-Cultural Psychology,* 1980, *11* (2), 153–172.

Crnic, K. A., Greenberg, M. T., Ragozin, A. S., Robinson, N. M., and Basham, R. "Effects of Stress and Social Support on Mothers and Premature and Full-Term Infants." *Child Development,* 1983, *54* (1), 209–217.

Crowell, J. A., and Feldman, S. S. "Mothers' Internal Models of Relationships and Children's Behavioral and Developmental Status: A Study of Mother-Child Interaction." *Child Development,* 1988, *59* (5), 1273–1285.

Crowell, J. A., and Feldman, S. S. "Mothers' Working Models of Attachment Relationships and Mother and Child Behavior During Separation and Reunion." *Developmental Psychology,* 1991, *27* (4), 597–605.

Dix, T. H., and Grusec, J. E. "Parent Attribution Processes in Child Socialization." In I. E. Sigel (ed.), *Parental Belief Systems: The Psychological Consequences for Children.* Hillsdale, N.J.: Erlbaum, 1985.

Dix, T. H., Ruble, D. N., and Zambarano, R. J. "Mothers' Implicit Theories of Discipline: Child Effects, Parent Effects, and the Attribution Process." *Child Development,* 1989, *60* (6), 1373–1391.

Donovan, W. L., Leavitt, L. A., and Walsh, R. O. "Maternal Self-Efficacy: Illusory Control and Its Effects on Susceptibility to Learned Helplessness." *Child Development,* 1990, *61* (5), 1638–1647.

Egeland, B., Jacobvitz, D., and Sroufe, L. A. "Breaking the Cycle of Abuse." *Child Development,* 1988, *59* (4), 1080–1088.

Fonagy, P., Steele, H., and Steele, M. "Maternal Representations of Attachment During Pregnancy Predict the Organization of Infant-Mother Attachment at One Year of Age." *Child Development,* 1991, *62* (5), 891–905.

Gfellner, B. M. "Culture and Consistency in Ideal and Actual Child-Rearing Practices: A Study of Canadian Indian and White Parents." *Journal of Comparative Family Studies,* 1990, *21* (3), 413–423.

Goodnow, J. J. "Change and Variation in Ideas About Childhood and Parenting." In I. E. Sigel (ed.), *Parental Belief Systems: The Psychological Consequences for Children.* Hillsdale, N.J.: Erlbaum, 1985.

Goodnow, J. J., and Collins, W. A. *Development According to Parents: The Nature, Sources, and Consequences of Parents' Ideas.* Hillsdale, N.J.: Erlbaum, 1990.

Grusec, J. E., Adam, E., and Mammone, N. "Mental Representations of Relationships, Parent Belief Systems, and Parenting Behavior." Paper presented at the biennial meeting of the Society for Research in Child Development, New Orleans, Apr. 1993.

Grusec, J. E., and Mammone, N. "Features and Sources of Parents' Attributions About Themselves and Their Children." In N. Eisenberg (ed.), *Review of Personality and Social Psychology,* in press.

Hess, R. D., Kashiwagi, K., Azuma, H., Price, C. G., and Dickson, W. P. "Maternal Expectations for Mastery of Developmental Tasks in Japan and the United States." *International Journal of Psychology,* 1980, *15* (4), 259–271.

Kaufman, J., and Zigler, E. "The Intergenerational Transmission of Child Abuse." In D. Cicchetti and V. Carlson (eds.), *Child Maltreatment: Theory and Research on the Causes and Consequences of Child Abuse and Neglect.* New York: Cambridge University Press, 1989.

Keller, H., Miranda, D., and Gauda, G. "The Naive Theory of the Infant and Some Maternal Attitudes." *Journal of Cross-Cultural Psychology,* 1984, *15* (2), 165–179.

Kelley, M. L., Power, T. G., and Wimbush, D. D. "Determinants of Disciplinary Practices in Low-Income Black Mothers." *Child Development,* 1992, *63* (3), 573–582.

Kelley, M. L., and Tseng, H. M. "Cultural Differences in Child-Rearing: A Comparison of

Immigrant Chinese and Caucasian American Mothers." *Journal of Cross-Cultural Psychology,* 1992, *23* (4), 444–455.

Larrance, D. T., and Twentyman, C. T. "Maternal Attributions and Child Abuse." *Journal of Abnormal Psychology,* 1983, *92* (5), 449–457.

McGillicuddy-DeLisi, A. V. "Parental Beliefs About Developmental Processes." *Human Development,* 1982, *25* (3), 192–200.

Main, M., and Goldwyn, R. "Adult Attachment Rating and Classification Systems." Unpublished manuscript, University of California at Berkeley, 1991.

Main, M., Kaplan, N., and Cassidy, J. "Security in Infancy, Childhood, and Adulthood: A Move to the Level of Representation." In I. Bretherton and E. Waters (eds.), *Growing Points of Attachment: Theory and Research.* Monographs of the Society for Research in Child Development, vol. 50, nos. 1–2 (serial no. 209). Chicago: University of Chicago Press, 1985.

Mash, E. J., and Johnston, C. "A Comparison of Mother-Child Interactions of Younger and Older Hyperactive and Normal Children." *Child Development,* 1982, *53* (5), 1371–1381.

Mash, E. J., and Johnston, C. "Parental Perceptions of Child Behavior Problems, Parenting Self-Esteem, and Mothers' Reported Stress in Younger and Older Hyperactive and Normal Children." *Journal of Consulting and Clinical Psychology,* 1983, *51* (1), 86–99.

Mash, E. J., and Johnston, C. "Determinants of Parenting Stress: Illustrations from Families of Hyperactive Children and Families of Physically Abused Children." *Journal of Clinical Child Psychology,* 1990, *19* (4), 313–328.

Moss, H. A., and Jones, S. J. "Relations Between Maternal Attitudes and Maternal Behavior as a Function of Social Class." In P. H. Leiderman, S. R. Tulkin, and A. Rosenfeld (eds.), *Culture and Infancy.* San Diego: Academic Press, 1977.

Murphy, D. A. "Constructing the Child: Relations Between Parents' Beliefs and Child Outcomes." *Developmental Review,* 1992, *12* (2), 199–232.

Ninio, A. "The Naive Theory of the Infant and Other Maternal Attitudes in Two Subgroups in Israel." *Child Development,* 1979, *50* (4), 976–980.

Sameroff, A. J., and Feil, L. A. "Parental Concepts of Development." In I. E. Sigel (ed.), *Parental Belief Systems: The Psychological Consequences for Children.* Hillsdale, N.J.: Erlbaum, 1985.

Sigel, I. E., McGillicuddy-DeLisi, A. V., and Goodnow, J. J. (eds.). *Parental Belief Systems: The Psychological Consequences for Children.* (2nd ed.) Hillsdale, N.J.: Erlbaum, 1992.

Sroufe, L. A., and Fleeson, J. "Attachment and the Construction of Relationships." In W. W. Hartup and Z. Rubin (eds.), *The Nature and Development of Relationships.* Hillsdale, N.J.: Erlbaum, 1985.

Teti, D. M., and Gelfand, D. M. "Behavioral Competence Among Mothers of Infants in the First Year: The Mediational Role of Maternal Self-Efficacy." *Child Development,* 1991, *62* (5), 918–929.

Trickett, P. K., and Susman, E. J. "Parental Perceptions of Child-Rearing Practices in Physically Abusive and Nonabusive Families." *Developmental Psychology,* 1988, *24* (2), 270–276.

Van IJzendoorn, M. H. "Intergenerational Transmission of Parenting: A Review of Studies in Non-Clinical Populations." *Developmental Review,* 1992, *12* (1), 76–99.

JOAN E. GRUSEC is professor of psychology at the University of Toronto.

PAUL HASTINGS is a doctoral candidate in psychology at the University of Toronto.

NORMA MAMMONE is a doctoral candidate in psychology at the University of Toronto.

Baumrind's typological model of parenting styles is a global characterization that varies along the dimensions of demandingness and responsiveness. A consideration of conceptions of parental authority in different conceptual domains adds greater specificity to the model and potentially contributes to the prediction of child competence and development.

Parenting Styles and Beliefs About Parental Authority

Judith G. Smetana

Typological models of parenting have a long history in developmental psychology. For nearly half a century, researchers have attempted to identify stable patterns of attitudes and behaviors on which parents characteristically differ (see Maccoby and Martin, 1983, for a review). The long-standing interest in defining different styles of parenting has been primarily predictive; researchers have sought constellations of parental behavior that can reliably predict a range of child outcomes (Maccoby and Martin, 1983). Only recently have researchers come to view parenting attitudes, beliefs, and evaluations as a legitimate and interesting topic of study in and of itself (see, for example, Goodnow, 1988; Goodnow and Collins, 1990; Sigel, McGillicuddy-DeLisi, and Goodnow, 1992).

Baumrind's (1971, 1988, 1991a, 1991b, 1991c) typology is currently the most widely employed model of parenting styles. According to Baumrind, parenting varies along the two orthogonal dimensions of demandingness and responsiveness, which, when crossed, yield four styles: *Authoritative* parents are both responsive and demanding. They exert consistent and firm control but provide clear explanations for their standards. These parents are loving, supportive, and encourage autonomy. *Authoritarian* parents, in contrast, are demanding but not responsive. They view obedience as a virtue and favor punitive responses when their children's beliefs or behavior conflict with their own standards of permissible conduct. These parents discourage verbal give-and-take and are not responsive to their children's needs. *Permissive* parents are responsive but not demanding. They are warm and allow considerable self-regulation of their activities. These parents make few maturity demands and do not insist that their children follow parentally defined standards. *Rejecting-*

neglecting parents are disengaged and neither demanding nor responsive; they are highly coercive but do not monitor their children's behavior.

These four parenting styles encompass both parents' attitudes and values about parenting and their beliefs about the nature of children, as well as the specific practices they employ to socialize their children. Parenting styles are seen as functionally stable over time. Because they are global characterizations of parental beliefs, attitudes, and behaviors, the context of behaviors is not directly relevant to the evaluation of parenting orientation.

Situational Variations in Parenting

There are three lines of research, briefly reviewed in the following sections, that suggest that parents' beliefs and behaviors are more contextually variable than the research on parenting styles suggests.

Parental Discipline. Research on parental discipline indicates that parents' responses to their children's misbehavior depend on the nature of the rules or standards that the children have violated. Parents have a large repertoire of disciplinary strategies. In some situations they employ power assertive techniques such as unexplained commands and punishment, whereas in other situations they use more cognitively oriented strategies such as reasoning and explanations (Grusec and Goodnow, 1994). Thus, the research suggests that parents' responses to transgressions are not consistent and that the choice of disciplinary strategy depends on the nature of the situation or transgression.

For instance, Grusec and Kuczynski (1980) found that mothers typically responded to hypothetical transgressions with power assertion. However, three transgressions pertaining to fairness, psychological harm, and children's safety all elicited responses primarily focusing on reasoning. Likewise, Zahn-Waxler and Chapman (1982) found that very young children's transgressions against people typically were associated with psychological discipline methods, such as parental reasoning and dramatizations of distress. Transgressions involving property destruction or lack of self-control, however, typically elicited parental power assertion, such as physical punishment or love withdrawal. Grusec, Dix, and Mills (1982) found that more serious transgressions elicited more persuasive reasoning (and more anger and upset in mothers) than did less serious transgressions. Finally, Trickett and Kuczynski (1986) found that transgressions pertaining to noncompliance or high-arousal behaviors (for instance, noisy, disruptive behavior or rough-and-tumble play) most frequently elicited requests for compliance or power-assertive responses. However, transgressions involving unprovoked aggression, destructiveness, violations of others' rights, or lapses in consideration for others, as well as conventional transgressions such as leaving clothes lying around, bad table manners, and coming home late, typically elicited reasoning.

Collectively, these studies suggest that situations "pull" for different types of parental responses. That is, misbehaviors involving psychological or physical harm to others (or the self), fair distribution, or violations of rights all appear to elicit more reasoning than situations involving disruptive or inappropriate violations of social norms. Kuczynski (1984) proposed that parents choose strategies for controlling behavior that are most appropriate to their socialization goals in particular situations. More specifically, he found that mothers are more nurturant, reason more, and provide a more diverse range of explanations when their goal is long-term rather than short-term compliance.

Domain-Specific Responses to Transgressions. The results of these studies can be better understood by considering research stemming from a domain-specificity model of social-cognitive development (Smetana, 1983; Turiel, 1983; Turiel and Davidson, 1986). According to this model, *morality,* which is defined as a matter pertaining to others' welfare, trust, or the equitable distribution of resources, is conceptually distinct from *social conventions,* which are defined as arbitrary, consensually agreed-on behavioral uniformities that vary within different social systems and include such issues as forms of address, manners, and dress. In turn, morality and convention are seen as distinct from *personal* issues, which are defined as issues that pertain only to the actor and, as such, are considered to be beyond the realm of conventional regulation and moral concern (Nucci, 1981; Nucci and Lee, 1993; Smetana, 1982, in press *a*). These three types of social knowledge are thought to be conceptually distinct in social development because they develop from different types of social interactions (Smetana, 1983; Turiel, 1983; Turiel, Killen, and Helwig, 1987).

The results of the aforementioned studies of parental discipline are consistent with the results of several observational studies of adult and child responses to naturally occurring moral and conventional transgressions. These studies indicate that adults generally reason and provide explanations in response to moral disputes such as hitting, pushing, and not sharing objects. In contrast, adults typically respond with power assertion to conventional transgressions; they issue commands to cease the behavior (without offering explanations) or punish the transgressor. Less frequently, adults respond to conventional transgressions by focusing on aspects of social organization, such as rules or statements regarding the disorder that the act creates. These responses have been observed among mothers and young children in the home (Dunn and Munn, 1987; Smetana, 1989b), as well as between adults and children in preschools and day cares (Much and Shweder, 1978; Nucci and Turiel, 1978; Smetana, 1984), in schools (Nucci and Nucci, 1982b), and on playgrounds (Nucci and Nucci, 1982a).

Conceptions of Parental Authority. These two lines of research focus on parental practices rather than beliefs. But a third and related line of research on adolescents' and parents' conceptions of parental authority focuses on parental beliefs. This research indicates that parents view their authority as bounded and dependent on the nature of the act. In this research, adolescents and parents evaluated the legitimacy of parental authority regarding moral, conventional, and personal issues (Smetana, 1988, 1993; Smetana and

Asquith, 1994; Tisak, 1986), as well as an additional category of acts referred to as prudential. Prudential issues are an aspect of the personal domain and refer to acts that have immediate, negative, and directly perceptible conse- quences to the self. Prudential issues typically pertain to safety, harm to the self, comfort, and health (Shweder, Turiel, and Much, 1981; Tisak, 1993; Tisak and Turiel, 1984).

The research indicates that from preadolescence through late adolescence, adolescents and their parents agree that parents should have the authority to regulate moral issues (such as not lying to parents, not stealing, and not harm- ing others), conventional issues (such as not cursing, being polite to parents, and using table manners), and prudential issues (such as drug and alcohol use and cigarette smoking). With increasing age, however, adolescents questioned parents' legitimate authority to regulate personal issues (such as choice of activ- ities, music, and hairstyles). Although parents also believed that adolescents should have greater autonomy regarding these issues as they grow older, ado- lescents viewed themselves as having greater autonomy than their parents were willing to grant them.

The research on disciplinary styles, adult responses to moral and con- ventional transgressions, and conceptions of parental authority all suggest that parenting beliefs and styles may be affected by the nature of the act under con- sideration. Yet research on parenting styles has not systematically examined how parenting styles are affected by the type of situations that require parental intervention. Although differences in how parents conceptualize and enforce rules and authority in the family are implicit in the definitions of the parent- ing styles, the styles are seen as global and content-free. A consideration of par- enting styles in terms of different domains of parental authority provides more fine-grained analyses of parenting beliefs.

Parenting Styles and Conceptions of Parental Authority

Elsewhere (Smetana, in press *a*), I proposed that parents' appeals to social con- ventions (societal laws, cultural norms or conventions, or more idiosyncratic family rules and expectations) serve to maintain social order, facilitate social interaction, and facilitate children's effective participation in society. In con- trast, children's appeals to personal jurisdiction serve to increase their agency, or enlarge their sphere of personal action, and thus serve an individuating function in development. Likewise, demandingness and responsiveness can be seen to reflect the balance between societal demands and the individual (Dar- ling and Steinberg, 1993). That is, demandingness can be conceptualized in terms of parents' willingness to make and enforce moral and conventional rules, whereas responsiveness indexes parents' willingness to recognize their children's individuality and autonomy. Thus, differences among authoritarian, authoritative, and permissive parents can be reconceptualized in terms of how they draw boundaries among moral, conventional, and personal issues.

The results of a recent study (Smetana, in press *b*) illustrate the relations between Baumrind's authoritarian, authoritative, and permissive parenting styles and parents' conceptions of legitimate parental authority in different conceptual domains. The sample consisted of 108 mothers and 92 fathers from 110 primarily intact (84 percent), white (89 percent), lower-middle-class families with sixth, eighth, and tenth graders.

Parents were asked to evaluate twenty-four hypothetical moral, conventional, prudential, and personal issues. An additional type of item, referred to as mixed or multifaceted, also was included to provide a more detailed assessment of how parents with different parenting orientations drew boundaries between legitimate parental authority and adolescents' personal jurisdiction. The multifaceted items pertained to issues that contain both conventional and personal components and that thus overlap the boundaries of the two domains. For instance, whether or not an adolescent cleans her room can be conceptualized as personal to the extent that the room is viewed as the adolescent's private territory and up to her to control, whereas keeping the room tidy can be seen as a conventional issue to the extent that the room is seen as part of the house and subject to parental standards for cleanliness and order. Previous research has indicated that adolescents and parents typically differ in how they conceptualize such issues and that these different interpretations cause conflict between adolescents and parents (Smetana, 1989a). In this study, multifaceted issues included issues of authority in the home (not cleaning one's room or not putting clothes away), taste (a boy wearing an earring), and friendships (such as seeing a friend that parents do not like or going to a movie alone with a boyfriend or girlfriend). Parenting style was assessed on a thirty-item questionnaire; parents rated, on 5-point Likert scales, statements based on Baumrind's (1971) definitions of permissive, authoritarian, and authoritative parental prototypes (Buri, 1989, 1991; Buri, Louiselle, Misukanis, and Mueller, 1988). Items pertaining to rejecting-neglecting parenting were not included in the scale and therefore this parenting style was not examined in this study.

Domain-Differentiated Conceptions of Parental Authority. As expected, parents' conceptions of parental authority differed as a function of parenting style. Differences were primarily over the boundaries of the personal domain. Permissive parents constructed the adolescents' personal domain more broadly than did other parents, whereas authoritarian parents were more restrictive.

Figures 2.1 and 2.2 graphically depict parents' judgments of their legitimate authority and their duty and obligation to make rules about each type of issue. As the figures demonstrate, except for personal issues, the majority of parents viewed parents as having both the legitimate authority and the obligation to make rules about all issues. With increasing frequency, mixed, conventional, prudential, and moral issues were viewed as legitimately regulated by parents and as obligatory in terms of parental rule making. In contrast, the majority of parents did not consider parents to have the legitimate authority or obligation to make rules regarding personal issues.

Both sets of judgments differed as a function of parenting style, however.

Figure 2.1. Percentage Distribution of Parents' Judgments of Their Legitimate Authority to Make Rules as a Function of Parenting Style

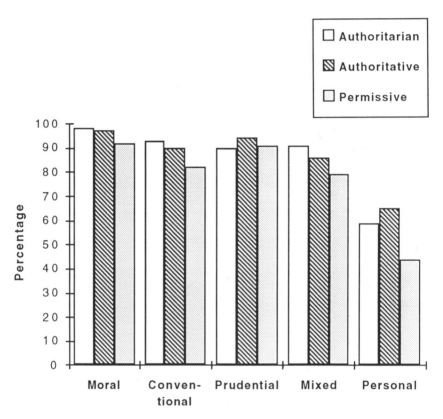

Authoritarian and authoritative parents judged all acts to be more legitimately regulated by parents than did permissive parents. Furthermore, authoritarian parents viewed rules regarding conventional and mixed issues as more obligatory than did all other parents. Unlike other parents, authoritarian parents also did not differentiate among the obligatoriness of moral, conventional, and mixed rules. As moral issues are considered prescriptive and obligatory, whereas conventional rules are not (Turiel, 1983), these findings indicate that authoritarian parents moralized nonmoral issues. Although the majority of parents judged that parents are not obligated to make rules about personal issues, authoritative and authoritarian parents viewed rules regarding personal issues to be more obligatory than did permissive parents.

Parents also were asked to sort items as "always wrong, whether or not parents say so," "wrong only if parents say so," and "not an issue of right or wrong—should be up to the individual to decide." These categories have been used in previous research to indicate the moral, conventional, and personal domains, respectively (Nucci, 1981; Smetana, 1981, 1988, 1993; Smetana and

**Figure 2.2. Percentage Distribution of Parents' Judgments
of Their Obligation to Make Rules as a Function of Parenting Style**

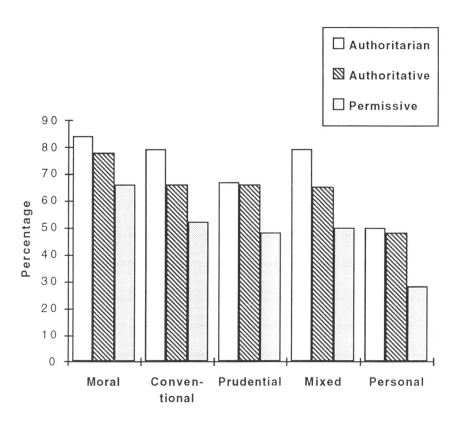

Asquith, 1994). The findings for parents' sorting of issues as up to the adolescent to decide, graphically depicted in Figure 2.3, are illuminating. As can be seen, only personal issues were sorted in this category in significant frequencies. However, except for moral issues, which were rarely treated as personal by any of the parents, permissive parents sorted all issues in this category more than did other parents.

The results of this study are consistent with Baumrind's descriptions of parenting styles (Baumrind, 1978, 1991a, 1991c). Permissive parents were found to be highly responsive to adolescents' desires for autonomy and not very demanding in their socialization attempts, whereas authoritarian parents were found to be more restrictive than other parents in constructing the boundaries of parents' legitimate authority. However, the domain assessment of parents' conceptions of parental authority also added greater specificity to Baumrind's parenting categories.

Domain categorizations are not static or inherent to the events themselves but rather are constructed out of interactions (Turiel, Killen, and Helwig, 1987;

**Figure 2.3. Percentage Distribution of Parents'
Sorting of Issues as Personal as a Function of Parenting Style**

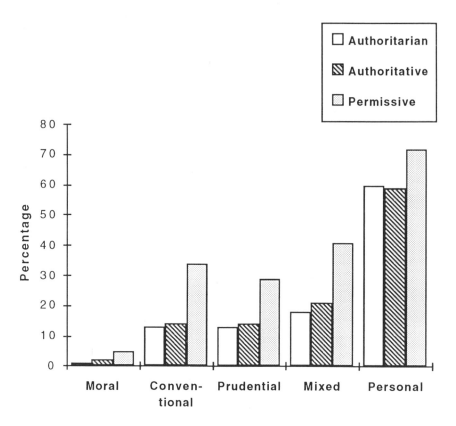

Turiel, Smetana, and Killen, 1991). More specifically, according to the domain view, the boundaries between conventional and personal issues and the content of the personal domain are relatively permeable and vary as a function of culture and development (Nucci, in press; Nucci and Lee, 1993; Smetana, in press *a*). Within American culture, preschool children (Smetana, 1986; Tisak, 1993) and their parents (Nucci and Smetana, 1994; Nucci and Weber, in press) view some issues as personal for children. However, what is considered to be under children's personal jurisdiction increases in scope with age, particularly during adolescence (Smetana, 1988, 1993; Smetana and Asquith, 1994).

The findings suggest that permissive parents construct wider boundaries of adolescents' personal autonomy vis-à-vis personal and mixed issues than do other parents of same-age children. In contrast to Baumrind (1978), who asserted that permissive parents are as vigilant as other parents in protecting their children's health and safety, permissive parents were also found to be more lenient than other parents in their judgments about issues pertaining to adolescents' welfare (that is, moral issues) and their health and safety (that is, prudential issues). Thus, permissive parents inappropriately relinquished their socializing role by granting adolescents personal autonomy over issues that cause intrinsic harm to others (that is, moral issues) and to the self (that is, prudential issues), are socially regulated (that is, conventional issues), or are ambiguously conventional (that is, mixed issues). By treating these issues as largely personal for adolescents, permissive parents may give adolescents more autonomy than they are capable of handling and may fail to convey appropriate societal standards, norms, and expectations.

Because morality pertains to issues that have intrinsic consequences for others' rights or welfare, less flexibility in the definition of these events would be expected. Indeed, research indicates that from very early ages onward, children (and their parents) treat moral events as moral on a variety of criteria (Nucci and Turiel, 1978; Smetana, 1981, 1983; Tisak, 1993; Turiel, 1983; Turiel and Davidson, 1986). In this study, however, authoritarian parents overgeneralized morality to nonmoral (conventional) issues. Thus, the overcontrol that is characteristic of authoritarian parents (Baumrind, 1978) was evidenced here in a tendency to moralize parental authority and to treat both moral and conventional issues as more obligatory than do other parents. Thus, authoritarian parents may oversocialize their children and fail to grant adolescents personal autonomy over issues that are typically treated as personal in this culture. It is not surprising that adolescents of authoritarian and permissive parents are less competent than adolescents of authoritative parents and are rarely seen as optimally competent (Baumrind, 1991a).

Only authoritative parents maintained clear and appropriate boundaries among moral, conventional, and personal issues in their judgments and justifications. Authoritative parents granted adolescents autonomy over a rather limited range of personal issues but did not grant them autonomy over multifaceted, friendship, and prudential issues. Instead, authoritative parents focused on the conventional, psychological, or prudential components of these issues. By articulating clearly the societal or welfare concerns that complex issues raise, authoritative parents may facilitate adolescents' understanding of the limits or boundaries of their personal autonomy. Defining those boundaries either too permissively or too rigidly may deprive adolescents and parents of the opportunity to negotiate appropriate boundaries, which, in turn, may be detrimental to adolescent development.

Perceptions of Parenting Styles

Baumrind (1991a) utilized a multimethod approach to assessing parenting styles that includes behavioral observations, parent rating scales, and psychologists' Q-Sorts. A more common strategy, however, particularly with adolescents, has been to obtain adolescents' reports of parents' parenting styles (for example, Dornbusch and others, 1987; Durbin, Darling, Steinberg, and Brown, 1993; Steinberg, Elmen, and Mounts, 1989; Steinberg, Lamborn, and Dornbusch, 1992; Steinberg, Mounts, Lamborn, and Dornbusch, 1991). Although adolescents' perceptions may be a more important predictor of adolescent out-comes than are parents' reports (Buri, 1989), surprisingly little research has compared parents' and adolescents' perceptions of parents' parenting styles. In my study (Smetana, in press b), both adolescents' and parents' reports of par-enting style were obtained. Parents' and adolescents' perceptions of parents' parenting styles were found to differ markedly.

Chi-square analyses revealed that adolescents viewed both their mothers and fathers as either permissive or authoritarian. Adolescents viewed 44 per-cent of mothers and 40 percent of fathers as permissive and 29 percent of mothers and 37 percent of fathers as authoritarian. In contrast, mothers (48 percent) and fathers (36 percent) predominantly viewed themselves as author-itative, and, less frequently, as permissive (12 percent of mothers and 18 per-cent of fathers) or authoritarian (11 percent of mothers and 29 percent of fathers). These findings indicate a large disjuncture between parents' attitudes and socialization goals and the way in which these are perceived by adoles-cents. It is not clear, however, whether these findings reflect a discrepancy between parents' parenting beliefs and their actual parenting practices or whether parents act on their beliefs but their attitudes and behaviors are mis-interpreted by their adolescents.

Discrepancies as Functional for Development. One interpretation of these findings is that adolescents' and parents' different goals lead adolescents to systematically distort their perceptions of their parents. The analyses of con-ceptions of parental authority indicated that authoritative parents were more restrictive than permissive parents but less restrictive than authoritarian par-ents in drawing the boundaries of adolescents' personal jurisdiction. However, adolescents of authoritative parents did not differ from other adolescents in their parental authority judgments (as assessed on a number of criteria). Regardless of their parents' parenting style, adolescents desired more auton-omy than their parents granted them. Thus, the authoritative parents con-structed considerably wider boundaries of their legitimate authority than did their adolescents.

One of the major developmental tasks of adolescence is to become increasingly emancipated from parental rules and perspectives. Thus, the ten-sion of adolescents' appeals to personal jurisdiction over issues that parents consider to be social-conventional may provide a mechanism for the renego-tiation of the boundaries between parental authority and individual authority over the self that is normative for this developmental period. Parents of ado-lescents must shift from viewing a variety of issues as conventional and legiti-mately subject to their authority to granting the adolescent increasing autonomy over them. Parents' appeals to social convention, adolescents' rejec-tions of their parents' perspectives, and parents' reinterpretation of conven-tions as legitimately within adolescents' sphere of jurisdiction form a continual dialectic in which the boundaries of parental authority are subtly transformed (Smetana, in press a). In turn, this suggests that there may be optimal discrepancies between adolescents' and parents' views that are functional for adolescent development.

Authoritative parents may be more successful in renegotiating parental authority because their adherence to appropriate boundaries between parental and societal standards and adolescents' personal jurisdiction may provide the optimal tension for this dialectical process to proceed. Nevertheless, authoritative parents' greater restrictiveness, relative to adolescents' desires, may promote the perception that they are authoritarian. In contrast, in granting adolescents too much autonomy too early in development, permissive parents may bias the tension between individual and societal perspectives too much toward the developing adolescent. Finally, in overextending societal perspectives to personal issues, authoritarian parents may not relinquish authority in developmentally appropriate ways. Because authoritative parenting also involves the use of reasoning and explanations and a responsiveness to adolescents' perspectives, these parents may be more willing to negotiate the boundaries of parental authority. Negotiation may provide a context for parents and children to articulate and discuss divergent perspectives, which, in turn, lead to changes in those perspectives. That is, authoritative parents may be more effective than other parents in renegotiating and reevaluating the limits of their authority and the boundaries of adolescents' personal jurisdiction. This view is consistent with recent research proposing that adolescent-parent conflict in the context of warm and close relationships is functional for adolescent development (Collins, 1990; Collins and Laursen, 1992; Grotevant and Cooper, 1986; Smetana, in press a; Steinberg, 1990).

Parenting Styles as Multidimensional. Beliefs about different domains of parental authority and parents' beliefs about parenting, as assessed here, do not measure the totality of parenting styles. As others (Darling and Steinberg, 1993; Maccoby and Martin, 1983) have noted, parenting styles entail other attributes, such as warmth, coerciveness, firm control, and communicativeness. Thus, another explanation for the discrepancies between adolescents' and parents' views of parenting style is that adolescents and parents draw on different types of information in making their evaluations. That is, parents' perceptions of their parenting style may be informed by their attitudes about child rearing, their views of children, and their judgments regarding parental authority. Children, on the other hand, may be less familiar with their parents' attitudes and values and instead may attend more to the way in which such attitudes and values are conveyed.

Nevertheless, discrepancies between parents' and adolescents' beliefs are consistent with a great deal of previous research on parental social cognition (Goodnow, 1988) and adolescent-parent authority relations (Smetana, 1988, 1989a, 1993). They raise questions about whose perceptions should be studied and how discrepancies should be treated (Carlton-Ford, Paikoff, and Brooks-Gunn, 1991). Researchers relying on adolescents' perceptions of parenting style have argued that it does not matter whether adolescents' perceptions are veridical or not because their perceptions have psychological reality for them.

Directions for Future Research

The findings discussed here, as well as the larger body of research on parenting styles, raise several unanswered questions that should be addressed in further research.

Antecedents of Parenting Beliefs. The analyses discussed here indicate that beliefs about parenting style are informed by examining beliefs about parental authority in different conceptual domains. But the source of the different beliefs about parenting still remain to be identified. Future research needs to examine the antecedents of parenting orientations in parents' values, socialization goals, beliefs about children, and beliefs about the efficacy of different child rearing practices. No doubt, there is both historical and cultural variability in these beliefs, as Youniss (this volume) convincingly demonstrates. However, the individual factors that lead to different orientations within a particular culture and time have not yet been specified.

Wainryb (1991) indicated that moral judgments are affected by the informational assumptions that inform or underlie judgments and that what have been described as differences in moral judgments can be attributed more appropriately to differences in informational assumptions. This distinction may be useful here. Parenting styles can be seen as differences in parents' informational assumptions about effective child rearing and normative child development. These assumptions may affect parents' evaluative judgments regarding children's behavior.

Relations Between Parenting Beliefs and Parenting Practices. Both parenting styles and parental authority have been conceptualized and discussed in this chapter in terms of parental beliefs. But to understand parenting, it is important to determine whether different parenting beliefs are related to parents' actual parenting practices. Darling and Steinberg (1993) distinguished between parenting practices, defined by specific content and socialization goals, and parenting styles, which provide the context in which particular parenting practices are enforced. Thus, in their model, parenting styles include the broader dimensions of warmth, coerciveness, and communicativeness (Darling and Steinberg, 1993; Maccoby and Martin, 1983).

The view of parenting styles described in this chapter is consistent with Darling and Steinberg's (1993) call for greater specificity in defining the different components of parenting. However, the research discussed here suggests that parental beliefs should be separated from the way in which these beliefs are communicated (or what Darling and Steinberg refer to as parenting style). Future research needs to examine the associations among different parenting beliefs, the emotional climate and manner in which beliefs are conveyed, and actual parenting practices.

Parenting Beliefs, Parenting Practices, and Child Behavior and Development. Finally, we know little about how different components of parenting, including parenting beliefs, parental practices, and the way in which these are conveyed, are related to child development and behavior. Future research must examine the processes by which parenting influences child development in different contexts. Separating the different components of parenting and considering domain-differentiated beliefs about parental authority might yield a clearer understanding of the role of parenting beliefs and behaviors in child development.

References

Baumrind, D. "Current Patterns of Parental Authority." *Developmental Psychology Monographs,* 1971, *4* (1, pt. 2).

Baumrind, D. "Parental Disciplinary Patterns and Social Competence in Children." *Youth and Society,* 1978, *9* (2), 239–276.

Baumrind, D. "Rearing Competent Children." In W. Damon (ed.), *Child Development Today and Tomorrow.* San Francisco: Jossey-Bass, 1988.

Baumrind, D. "Effective Parenting During the Early Adolescent Transition." In P. A. Cowan and E. M. Hetherington (eds.), *Advances in Family Research.* Vol. 2. Hillsdale, N.J.: Erlbaum, 1991a.

Baumrind, D. "The Influence of Parenting Style on Adolescent Competence and Substance Use." *Journal of Early Adolescence,* 1991b, *11* (1), 56–95.

Baumrind, D. "Parenting Styles and Adolescent Development." In J. Brooks-Gunn, R. Lerner, and A. C. Peterson (eds.), *The Encyclopedia of Adolescence.* New York: Garland, 1991c.

Buri, J. R. "Self-Esteem and Appraisals of Parental Behavior." *Journal of Adolescent Research,* 1989, *4* (1), 33–49.

Buri, J. R. "Parental Authority Questionnaire." *Journal of Personality Assessment,* 1991, *57* (1), 110–119.

Buri, J. R., Louiselle, P. A., Misukanis, T. M., and Mueller, R. A. "Effects of Parental Authoritarianism and Authoritativeness on Self-Esteem." *Personality and Social Psychology Bulletin,* 1988, *14* (2), 271–282.

Carlton-Ford, S. L., Paikoff, R. L., and Brooks-Gunn, J. "Methodological Issues in the Study of Divergent Views of the Family." In R. L. Paikoff (ed.), *Shared Views in the Family During Adolescence.* New Directions for Child Development, no. 51. San Francisco: Jossey-Bass, 1991.

Collins, W. A. "Parent-Child Relationships in the Transition to Adolescence: Continuity and Change in Interaction, Affect, and Cognition." In R. Montemayor, G. R. Adams, and T. P. Gullotta (eds.), *Advances in Adolescent Development.* Vol. 2: *From Childhood to Adolescence: A Transitional Period?* Newbury Park, Calif.: Sage, 1990.

Collins, W. A., and Laursen, B. "Conflict and Relationships During Adolescence." In C. U. Shantz and W. W. Hartup (eds.), *Conflict in Child and Adolescent Development.* New York: Cambridge University Press, 1992.

Darling, N., and Steinberg, L. "Parenting Style as Context: An Integrative Model." *Psychological Bulletin,* 1993, *113* (3), 487–496.

Dornbusch, S. M., Ritter, P. L., Leiderman, P. O., Roberts, D. F., and Fraleigh, M. J. "The Relation of Parenting Style to Adolescent School Performance." *Child Development,* 1987, *58* (5), 1244–1257.

Dunn, J., and Munn, P. "The Development of Justifications in Disputes." *Developmental Psychology,* 1987, *23* (6), 781–798.

Durbin, D. D., Darling, N., Steinberg, L., and Brown, B. B. "Parenting Style and Peer Group Orientation Among European-American Adolescents." *Journal of Research on Adolescence,* 1993, *3* (1), 87–100.

Goodnow, J. J. "Parents' Ideas, Actions, and Feelings: Models and Methods from Developmental and Social Psychology." *Child Development,* 1988, *59* (2), 286–320.

Goodnow, J. J., and Collins, W. A. *Development According to Parents: The Nature, Sources, and Consequences of Parents' Ideas.* Hillsdale, N.J.: Erlbaum, 1990.

Grotevant, H. D., and Cooper, C. R. "Individuation in Family Relationships: A Perspective on Individual Differences in the Development of Identity and Role-Taking in Adolescence." *Human Development,* 1986, *29* (2), 82–100.

Grusec, J. E., Dix, T., and Mills, R. "The Effects of Type, Severity, and Victim of Children's Transgressions on Maternal Discipline." *Canadian Journal of Behavioural Science,* 1982, *14* (4), 276–289.

Grusec, J. E., and Goodnow, J. J. "The Impact of Parental Discipline Methods on the Child's Internalization of Values: A Reconceptualization of Current Points of View." *Developmental Psychology,* 1994, *30* (1), 4–19.

Grusec, J. E., and Kuczynski, L. "Direction of Effect in Socialization: A Comparison of the Parent's Versus the Child's Behavior as Determinants of Disciplinary Techniques." *Developmental Psychology,* 1980, *16* (1), 1–9.

Kuczynski, L. "Socialization Goals and Mother-Child Interaction: Strategies for Long-Term and Short-Term Compliance." *Developmental Psychology,* 1984, *20* (6), 1061–1073.

Maccoby, E. E., and Martin, J. "Socialization in the Context of the Family: Parent-Child Interaction." In E. M. Hetherington (ed.), *Handbook of Child Psychology.* Vol. 4: *Socialization, Personality, and Social Development.* New York: Wiley, 1983.

Much, N., and Shweder, R. A. "Speaking of Rules: The Analysis of Culture in Breach." In W. Damon (ed.), *Moral Development.* New Directions for Child Development, no. 2. San Francisco: Jossey-Bass, 1978.

Nucci, L. P. "The Development of Personal Concepts: A Domain Distinct from Moral or Societal Concepts." *Child Development,* 1981, *52* (1), 114–121.

Nucci, L. P. "Morality and Personal Freedom." In T. Brown, E. Turiel, and E. Reed (eds.), *Knowledge and Values.* Hillsdale, N.J.: Erlbaum, in press.

Nucci, L. P., and Lee, J. Y. "Morality and Personal Autonomy." In G. G. Noam and T. Wren (eds.), *The Moral Self: Building a Better Paradigm.* Cambridge, Mass.: MIT Press, 1993.

Nucci, L. P., and Nucci, M. S. "Children's Responses to Moral and Social-Conventional Transgressions in Free-Play Settings." *Child Development,* 1982a, *53* (4), 1337–1342.

Nucci, L. P., and Nucci, M. S. "Children's Social Interactions in the Context of Moral and Conventional Transgressions." *Child Development,* 1982b, *53* (2), 403–412.

Nucci, L. P., and Smetana, J. G. "Mothers' Reasoning About Their Children's Personal Autonomy." Unpublished manuscript, College of Education, University of Illinois at Chicago, 1994.

Nucci, L. P., and Turiel, E. "Social Interactions and the Development of Social Concepts in Preschool Children." *Child Development,* 1978, *49* (2), 400–407.

Nucci, L. P., and Weber, E. K. "Social Interactions in the Home and the Development of Young Children's Conceptions of the Personal." *Child Development,* in press.

Shweder, R. A., Turiel, E., and Much, N. "The Moral Intuitions of the Child." In J. H. Flavell and L. Ross (eds.), *Social-Cognitive Development: Frontiers and Possible Futures.* New York: Cambridge University Press, 1981.

Sigel, I. E., McGillicuddy-DeLisi, A. V., and Goodnow, J. J. (eds.). *Parental Belief Systems: The Psychological Consequences for Children.* (2nd ed.) Hillsdale, N.J.: Erlbaum, 1992.

Smetana, J. G. "Reasoning in the Personal and Moral Domains: Adolescent and Young Adult Women's Decision Making Regarding Abortion." *Journal of Applied Developmental Psychology,* 1981, *3* (2), 211–226.

Smetana, J. G. *Concepts of Self and Morality: Women's Reasoning About Abortion.* New York: Praeger, 1982.

Smetana, J. G. "Social-Cognitive Development: Domain Distinctions and Coordinations." *Developmental Review,* 1983, *3* (1), 131–147.

Smetana, J. G. "Toddlers' Social Interactions Regarding Moral and Conventional Transgressions." *Child Development,* 1984, *55* (5), 1767–1776.

Smetana, J. G. "Preschool Children's Conceptions of Sex-Role Transgressions." *Child Development,* 1986, *57* (4), 862–871.

Smetana, J. G. "Adolescents' and Parents' Conceptions of Parental Authority." *Child Development,* 1988, *59* (2), 321–335.

Smetana, J. G. "Adolescents' and Parents' Reasoning About Actual Family Conflict." *Child Development,* 1989a, *60* (5), 1052–1067.

Smetana, J. G. "Toddlers' Social Interactions in the Context of Moral and Conventional Transgressions in the Home." *Developmental Psychology,* 1989b, *25* (4), 499–508.

Smetana, J. G. "Conceptions of Parental Authority in Divorced and Married Mothers and Their Adolescents." *Journal of Research on Adolescence,* 1993, *3* (1), 19–39.

Smetana, J. G. "Context, Conflict, and Constraint in Adolescent-Parent Authority Relationships." In M. Killen and D. Hart (eds.), *Morality in Everyday Life: Developmental Perspectives.* New York: Cambridge University Press, in press *a.*

Smetana, J. G. "Parental Style and Conceptions of Parental Authority During Adolescence." *Child Development,* in press *b.*

Smetana, J. G., and Asquith, P. "Adolescents' and Parents' Conceptions of Parental Authority and Adolescent Autonomy." *Child Development,* 1994, *65* (3), 1143–1158.

Steinberg, L. "Interdependency in the Family: Autonomy, Conflict, and Harmony." In S. S. Feldman and G. R. Elliot (eds.), *At the Threshold: The Developing Adolescent.* Cambridge, Mass.: Harvard University Press, 1990.

Steinberg, L., Elmen, D. J., and Mounts, N. S. "Authoritative Parenting, Psychosocial Maturity, and Academic Success Among Adolescents." *Child Development,* 1989, *60* (6), 1424–1436.

Steinberg, L., Lamborn, S. D., and Dornbusch, S. M. "Impact of Parenting Practices on Adolescent Achievement: Authoritative Parenting, School Involvement, and Encouragement to Succeed." *Child Development,* 1992, *63* (5), 1266–1281.

Steinberg, L., Mounts, N. S., Lamborn, S. D., and Dornbusch, S. M. "Authoritative Parenting and Adolescent Adjustment Across Varied Ecological Niches." *Journal of Research on Adolescence,* 1991, *1* (1), 19–36.

Tisak, M. "Children's Conceptions of Parental Authority." *Child Development,* 1986, *57* (1), 166–176.

Tisak, M. "Preschool Children's Judgments of Moral and Personal Events Involving Physical Harm and Property Damage." *Merrill-Palmer Quarterly,* 1993, *39* (3), 375–390.

Tisak, M., and Turiel, E. "Children's Conceptions of Moral and Prudential Rules." *Child Development,* 1984, *55* (3), 1030–1039.

Trickett, P. K., and Kuczynski, L. "Children's Misbehaviors and Parental Discipline Strategies in Abusive and Nonabusive Families." *Developmental Psychology,* 1986, *22* (1), 115–123.

Turiel, E. *The Development of Social Knowledge: Morality and Convention.* New York: Cambridge University Press, 1983.

Turiel, E., and Davidson, P. "Heterogeneity, Inconsistency, and Asynchrony in the Development of Cognitive Structures." In I. Levin (ed.), *Stage and Structure: Reopening the Debate.* Norwood, N.J.: Ablex, 1986.

Turiel, E., Killen, M., and Helwig, C. "Morality: Its Structure, Functions, and Vagaries." In J. Kagan and S. Lamb (eds.), *The Emergence of Morality in Young Children.* Chicago: University of Chicago Press, 1987.

Turiel, E., Smetana, J. G., and Killen, M. "Social Contexts in Social Cognitive Development."

In J. L. Gewirtz and W. M. Kurtines (eds.), *Handbook of Moral Behavior and Development.* Vol. 2. Hillsdale, N.J.: Erlbaum, 1991.

Wainryb, C. "Understanding Differences in Moral Judgments: The Role of Informational Assumptions." *Child Development,* 1991, 62 (4), 840–851.

Zahn-Waxler, C., and Chapman, M. "Immediate Antecedents of Caretakers' Methods of Discipline." *Child Psychiatry and Human Development,* 1982, 12 (2), 179–192.

JUDITH G. SMETANA *is professor of education, psychology, and pediatrics at the University of Rochester, Rochester, New York.*

If parents' child rearing practices and beliefs are to be understood, they are best viewed in their societal and historical context. Studies that illustrate the value of viewing parents in social context are reviewed and discussed and a way for psychologists to construe society as an interindividual construction is described.

Rearing Children for Society

James Youniss

The aim of this chapter is to enrich the literature on parents' beliefs by showing the importance of parents' understanding of society in their treatment and views of children and childhood. The chapter starts with a commentary on the child rearing literature of the 1950s and 1960s, when psychological and sociological approaches took separate paths. Psychologists tended to focus on the ways in which disciplinary actions conformed with principles of learning through which general behaviors were acquired. In contrast, sociologists sought to understand how child rearing practices were designed to prepare children for success in particular societal contexts.

The chapter then moves to the last decade, when psychologists began to acknowledge that child rearing practices were founded on parents' beliefs and knowledge. This insight led to studies of the cognitive processes that parents brought to the child rearing function. However, these studies of parents' cognition may be heading toward too narrow a focus on microprocesses in which parents and children exchange thoughts in an ongoing series of calculations, and reappraisals, as each tries to direct the other. It is better to balance this focus with a broader perspective on the sociological and historical context from which parents' rearing practices arise. From this perspective, practices can be seen as preparations for children's successful entry into society. This is to acknowledge that parents' understanding of society is essential to their practices and beliefs and gives them a definable goal beyond personal preference or children's well-being.

The chapter next offers a review of select studies that illustrate ways in which parents' societal positions differentiate their child rearing practices. A special review in this regard looks at changes in practices among parents who have immigrated from traditional to modern-technical societies. In the chapter's final section, a new way of conceptualizing the social context is considered. Rather than view society as a determinant macrostructure, it can be seen in terms of microsociological processes through which persons construct relationships, communities, and the society as a whole. If social reality comes about through interaction patterns that recursively define and sustain the broader social structure, then rearing practices, which consist in interaction patterns, prepare children for societal functioning while they reconstitute the structures of the society in which children are becoming members.

Sketch of 1950s and 1960s Child Rearing Literature

Studies of parents' beliefs are of relatively recent origin in the psychological literature, insofar as earlier research focused on correlations between parents' rearing practices and personality traits in children. That focus was based on a learning theory orientation in which personality traits, construed as behaviors, were seen to be acquired through the medium of parental practices. Parents' beliefs had no place in this approach because they were viewed as superfluous and would have required dealing with unobservable cognitive "acts" rather than observable behavior.

Nevertheless, some psychologists at the time were trying to include societal forces in the study of parent-child behavior, but their views were not generally pursued. For example, Baldwin (1955, p. 483) proposed that child rearing practices be studied "within a culture" and examined as patterns that "commonly occur in our culture." In Baldwin's view, the practice of encouraging children to reason on their own, as opposed to telling them directly what to do, was not a psychological absolute but rather followed from the dominant "democratic philosophy" of our culture (p. 516).

Bronfenbrenner (1958, 1961) also gave credit to the role of society when he tried to explain why rearing practices had changed historically during the twentieth century. He noted that since the 1920s, studies showed that middle-class parents had shifted from punitive methods of control to "psychological methods" of reasoning and appeals to guilt. He viewed this trend, and the narrowing gap between middle- and working-class practices, as signs of society's liberalization. He also attributed this trend to the increased management of children by mothers rather than fathers and to the advice of child rearing experts such as Dr. Benjamin Spock.

For Baldwin and Bronfenbrenner, parents were more than ciphers filling out parts in a mechanical learning process. They were members of society who understood the culture and were preparing children for adaptive functioning in it. In their view, no practice should be studied apart from the social context for which it was designed. Society's norms gave parents targets to achieve, and if these norms changed, then practices would change correspondingly because parents were resourceful and able to come up with strategies to help their children meet the altered conditions.

This line of thinking was not developed, probably because the then-dominant model of learning minimized the role of parents' cognition and obviated the need for cultural analysis. Insofar as learning was a universal process, energy could be devoted to the quest for "best practices" that would yield the "most desirable psychological traits." Research on practices was directed toward measures of dimensions such as warmth or control, loving or punitive styles, and types of practices such as induction or love withdrawal (Becker, 1964; Hoffman, 1970). On the child's side of the correlation, the desirability of certain traits, such as altruism, delay of gratification, and resistance to temptation (Kohlberg, 1969), was taken for granted since these traits were thought to be of universal, culturally noncontingent value.

This review is not intended as an indictment of psychological theories, but it is meant to represent the tenor of the field during a particular era. For a fuller perspective on these times, readers are directed to the project originally generated by John and Beatrice Whiting in the 1950s to assess child rearing across cultural settings. Whiting (1965, p. 4) described the aim of relating "personality to culture." In brief, "the researchers [on this project] viewed ecology, economics, and social and political organizations as setting the parameters for the behavior of the agents of child rearing. They viewed child behavior as an index of child personality and adult behavior and beliefs and values as indices of adult personality" (p. 5). One can see how this contextualization of learning was viewed as radical given the dominance of learning theory and its underlying assumption about the transcendent nature of psychological processes and traits.

A Sociological Counterpoint

Inkeles (1955) illustrated a sociologically based alternative to the learning model. Inkeles asked 330 Russian-born adults, who were living in the United States, to compare how their parents had reared them during the pre-1915 czarist regime with how they reared their own children. Clear differences between recollections of their own rearing and ways in which they had reared their own children were reported. They had been reared, more than they reared their children, to respect religious customs, strong family ties, and tradition. They, more so than their parents, had emphasized personalistic traits such as sincerity or justice. Further, they, more so than their parents, stressed learning, gaining knowledge, and taking interest in government.

The 1917 Bolshevik Revolution is a clear case of a drastically altered social context that placed parents in a position of choosing between habitual rearing practices and redesigned practices for new settings. Inkeles's results showed that parents did not persist in traditional habits but instead adapted to the new democratic context. What parents saw as worth promoting in their children differed from what had been fitting for themselves in the old setting. Given a choice, Inkeles (1955, p. 2) believed that parents would make "both purposive and unconscious adjustments in [their] child rearing practices, in mediating the influence of social change to [their] children and consequently in better adapting them for the changed social conditions they may next meet as adults."

For Inkeles and others, the goal of child rearing is to encourage the development of traits that enable children to be successful in society. Because societies change, desired traits necessarily vary with extant conditions. By implication, rearing practices have to vary with intended outcomes, which are open to alteration as parents' perceptions of the social context change.

Kohn's (1959, 1969) work on social class offered another way to address how society enters parents' rearing choices. He assumed that individuals view society differently according to their respective social class positions. His demonstration consisted in comparing middle- and working-class mothers' typical reactions to everyday situations that might elicit concern: wild play, fighting between siblings, and disobeying. In all three situations, working-class mothers were more likely than middle-class mothers to punish children, while middle-class mothers were more likely than working-class mothers to use psychological techniques of reasoning and discussion.

Kohn speculated that these differences originated in working- and middle-class parents' distinctive societal perspectives and values. Working-class mothers were seen to value the attainment of respect and thus to be prone to intervene to stop children's bad behavior. In contrast, middle-class parents were seen to value the internalization of standards, which children could use on their own as guides to situations as they arose. Hence, by this account, middle-class parents respond less to children's actions than to intentions, which signify the standards that children hold. Miller and Swanson (1960) described a similar distinction between "entrepreneurial" and "bureaucratic" fathers. Fathers who were small businessmen were seen as apt to use psychological techniques that encourage independence, while fathers in bureaucratic roles were seen to prefer direct control that enhances "getting along" with others.

In *The Lonely Crowd*, Riesman (1953) offered a broad framework for viewing the relation between parents' practices and the preparation of children for society. Riesman described changes in child rearing orientations that occurred as a result of large demographic changes in Western history. Eras differed in calling for different adjustments to society. Although parents in all eras shared the goal of preparing children for success, the means of success differed across the eras.

During the pre-industrial era, when birth and death rates were high, parents valued maintenance of tradition and customs. Hence, rearing practices stressed compliance and the maintenance of the communal order. The next demographic era, of decreased death rates and increased population, led to a focus on inner traits. In this inner-directed approach, rearing practices were geared to the internalization of honesty, hard work, patriotism, and the like.

The modern era of low birth and death rates, with a stabilized population, calls for other-directed rearing practices. Given rapid swings in values and customs, it would be dysfunctional to maintain tradition or demand inner traits that persist over time. Hence, parents promote sensitivity to cues in the social environment so that children can take readings of situations and judge which behaviors are appropriate for given moments. Other-directed persons are flexible, able to judge others, and adept at enlisting others in helping them get what they desire and need.

What Is Parents' Cognition About?

About a decade ago, psychologists substantively altered their outlook by recognizing that parents bring beliefs, goals, and cognitive abilities to the task of child rearing. The rapidity with which this new outlook developed probably attests a pent-up need to get beyond the learning orientation and to acknowledge that parents are cognitive agents (Goodnow, 1988; McGillicuddy-DeLisi, 1982; Sigel, 1985). After all, cognitive psychology had been thriving since the 1960s; it was clearly time for cognition, which had been granted to others, to be granted also to parents.

The initial studies that promoted this new outlook shifted focus from practice-outcome correlations to parents' beliefs about children, whence practices and outcomes emanated. McGillicuddy-DeLisi (1982), for instance, asked for parents' theories of how children learned and then observed parents interacting with children on a learning task. She reported that beliefs, more so than practices, were correlated with outcomes, indicating that parents have views about learning and know how to translate beliefs into strategic actions. Results showed also that beliefs are expressed through a variety of practices that are used as unfolding circumstances arise in the flow of parent-child interactions.

This work concurs with Kuczynski's (1984) important finding that rearing practices can be meaningfully segmented into long-term approaches and responses to immediate exigencies. Smart parenting involves both aspects because parents need to attend to emergent details of actual interactions while they work toward long-term goals. For instance, a parent who believes that children learn best when they construct their own solutions may be more apt to give hints and reasons than to intervene directly and force responses. Yet, if his or her child faced danger or embarrassment, this parent might directly intervene to get the child beyond the immediate situation and back to a safe mode where self-guidance can proceed.

In the intervening decade, studies of parents' cognition have expanded to address a variety of beliefs about children and childhood. It is evident that psychologists have recognized purpose and design in parents' rearing activities. Despite this advance, however, there is an unnecessary restrictiveness to these studies, which tend to be focused on the give-and-take between parent and child in the acquisition or remediation of behavior. While parents' calculations of children's intentions or abilities are important, they refer more to short-term exigencies than to long-range aims of parents' practices (Kuczynski, 1984).

If society were static and if everyone held the same station in it, a single set of traits might serve all children. But we know that society is not so stable and that individuals differ by class and other statuses. It follows that parents would be wise to tailor behavior to the particular social conditions they view as important. For instance, depending on social circumstances, physical aggression can be more or less appropriate and have multiple forms of appropriate expression. Or the ability to figure out rapidly what another person is about to do varies in usefulness according to the situations children are likely to encounter in their everyday environment. For instance, compare a middle-class child with children living by their own wits on the street. Aggression and quick reading of others undoubtedly play different roles in these children's lives and are probably developed to different degrees in knowledge and practice.

Specification of the different social situations for which children are being prepared helps to clarify the meaning of a behavior or trait. Studies of social-historical change and culture show the importance of such distinctions (Gadlin, 1978). A compelling historical illustration is found in a self-report by Rev. Francis Wayland, a Baptist minister and president of Brown University (McLoughlin, 1975). In 1831, Wayland published in *American Baptist Magazine* a description of his effort at "breaking the will" of his fifteen-month old son. When the boy refused to take bread from his father one morning, Rev. Wayland interpreted this act of disobedience as an indication that his son had not yet given up his will to God's. Wayland's antidote was to isolate and starve the boy until he gratefully took milk from his father. The procedure drew out over two days, when the boy finally softened and stopped inflicting "agony . . . upon himself" (McLoughlin, 1975, p. 36). Wayland said, "Since this event several slight revivals of his former temper have occurred, but they have all been easily subdued. His disposition is, as it never has been before, mild and obedient. He is . . . evidently much happier than he was when he was determined to have his own way" (p. 36).

From a contemporary perspective, this episode borders on abuse and implies insensitivity. In context, however, Wayland's actions and reasoning fit a shared communal perspective that was based on a Calvinist theology of predestination in which individuals could do nothing to save their souls. Because God had already decided who was to be saved, giving up one's will to God's was the only viable position a believer could take. Hence, it was Wayland's duty to help his son give up his own will and to accept God's will.

Another interesting case is in Miller and Sperry's (1987) study of interactions between single, working-class mothers and their two-year-old daughters about rules for expressing emotions. These mothers provoked daughters by teasing them unmercifully in trying to elicit a retaliatory aggressive reaction. Mothers insulted the girls with increasing intensity in trying to get them angry enough to strike back. Miller and Sperry's interpretation of these data relied on mothers' explanations, which explicitly referred to the social context. Mothers said that they were preparing their daughters to take care of themselves in a society that was hostile and harsh so that a rule of fighting back to protect oneself was adaptive. Striking out when not provoked was not allowable, but fighting back when sufficiently provoked was warranted and required. This example provides an obvious contrast with purported middle-class rules of emotional expression. The practices of these single, working-class mothers were shaped by an assessment of the social situations their daughters were likely to face. The rules that the mothers sought to instill were consciously and unconsciously practiced through episodes of challenge and defense for the context they knew.

Parents' interpretations of society are glaringly missing from psychological studies of parents' cognition. This is not to devalue the study of beliefs about children's learning but rather to suggest that parents' views of society are more than background and could tell us much about the choices parents make in rearing practices. Whether one hurries a child along or waits patiently for the child to achieve a milestone is as much a social as an individual matter. Parents may differ in temperament, with some not caring if their children are fast or slow achievers. But the very topic of rate of development is socially contingent and may not even come up in noncompetitive cultures. What we might take for granted as normal, say, fostering children's intelligence, has social value that is culturally rooted (Wertsch and Youniss, 1987). Parents' beliefs about children entail understandings of the social contexts they envision as relevant for their children. Strategies that parents adopt are conditioned by the kind of society and social class they believe applies to their children's eventual social adaptation (Whiting, 1963).

Immigration and Change in Parents' Orientation

Inkeles's (1955) study was built on the insight that, for many people, society is not a stable frame that is amenable to habitual behavior. In looking at immigrants, Inkeles hoped to learn how quickly parents switched their outlooks in new social contexts. A weakness of his study, however, was the use of retrospective recall of the subjects' own childhoods in comparison with the practices they used after becoming parents. This generational difference might be attributed to adaptivity, to faulty recall, or to the press of circumstances. Nevertheless, the study of immigration seems, in principle, useful for assessing how parents adapt rearing to fit the milieu that their children will enter. Fortunately, this topic has been well researched, and two sets of studies in this genre warrant review here.

Zivkovic (1990, in press) reported on two samples of Croatian parents in Croatia and North America. In the former, three hundred parents in Croatia were interviewed in 1987, when Croatia was part of the socialist Yugoslav state. Parents described rearing practices with adolescents pertaining to rules at home, schooling, peer behavior, and so on. Parents came from rural and urban settings and varied in status based on education, work, and Communist Party membership. Zivkovic found that parents differed in the degree to which they wanted adolescents to follow tradition or to pursue modern careers through further education. Parents who favored tradition said that they used directive rearing practices such as demanding compliance and punishing disobedience. These parents were likely to live in rural areas and to have had little formal schooling.

In contrast, urban, educated parents were much like middle-class parents in the United States in that they favored the practice of instilling self-directed-ness rather than compliance. These parents said that they used reasoning and other psychological techniques to guide adolescents toward desired goals. Finally, these parents consciously shared the rearing function with educators, whom they saw as essential to the adolescents' future careers. These parents promoted other-directedness by using school and other agents to supplement home training. In sum, Croatian parents from different settings manifested distinct approaches to rearing, with each approach appearing appropriate for that sector of Yugoslav society in which their adolescents were expected to fit.

Zivkovic (in press) studied three groups of Croatian parents who had migrated to North America. One group, which came from a rural district in Croatia, had relocated in an isolated section of urban northern New Jersey. Adults had retained many of their religious and ethnic traditions, spoke Croatian, and lived within a closed community. A contrast group of highly educated professionals had also immigrated to the United States after 1950. These individuals were spread across the country, did not live in ethnic enclaves, and had assimilated, but they still valued their Croatian heritage. A third group in Ontario, Canada, had migrated more recently and had working-class status. Of interest here are the first two groups.

Parents in the closed community had the highest scores on a scale that assessed ethnic identification and values. These parents also said that they wanted their children to retain Croatian identity, the language, dietary customs, and other ethnic traditions. On items from the Family Environment Scale (Moos and Moos, 1981), these parents claimed to have high family cohesion and medium conflict. On Kohn's (1969) measure of rearing, these parents preferred self-directedness over compliance, and on an open-ended question about schooling, they encouraged advanced education. In contrast, the assimilated professionals showed lower ethnic identity scores and had less desire that their children identify as Croatians. They claimed strong family cohesion and low family conflict. They also preferred self-directedness over compliance and promoted higher education for their children.

These results indicate that immigrants who differed in their levels of assimilation nevertheless adopted similar rearing practices for their children. Parents from the closed group appeared not to have assimilated but to have structured their lives around traditional values. They formed a community in which they were able to enact their ethnic identity on a daily, communal basis. Even though these parents wanted their adolescents to carry on their ethnic identity, they did not act like "traditional" parents in their rearing practices (Kohn, 1969; Zivkovic, 1990). They promoted self-directedness to the same degree as their assimilated counterparts and valued schooling, which enhanced assimilation.

The assimilated professionals had obviously taken a different route in their adaptation. They did not live in enclaves and more evenly balanced their Croatian background with an American identity. In child rearing, these parents looked much like parents from the closed group on self-directedness and schooling measures. Both groups appeared to design practices for the society in which their adolescents would eventually work, marry, and live as adults. Success in this society was enabled by having an education and being a self-directed, other-oriented individual. Hence, while parents from the two groups differed in the extent to which they accepted the host culture, they differed hardly at all in promoting behavior that would help their children become successful American citizens.

The second set of studies was reported by Nauck (1987, 1988, 1989a, 1989b) on Turkish parents living either in Turkey or Germany as immigrant guest workers. Nauck's results support Zivkovic's key finding that although adults vary in assimilation to the host culture, they display similar child rearing practices that tend toward the host culture's norms. This suggests that parents are sensitive to cultural differences and seek for their children behaviors that will suit adaptation to the host society.

In a base-line study on the "value of children," parents from eight countries, including Turkey and Germany, estimated benefits they expected to derive from having children (Nauck, 1989b). Over 70 percent of the Turkish parents in Turkey had a utilitarian view, which valued the wages that children added to family income and the security they could bring parents in old age. Only 12 percent of the German parents in Germany valued these functions. Further, 22 percent of the Turkish parents valued watching their children grow up, and 9 percent valued having their children become independent adults; respective figures for German parents were 73 percent and 51 percent. These results show that children's value varies with formal societal differences, such as whether a society has a policy for old-age insurance.

These findings are supported by data on fertility for Turkish women who immigrated to Germany at different phases of their family life cycles (Nauck, 1987). The lowest fertility rates were found in women who migrated before they were married or after marriage, but before they each had their first child. Fertility rates went up systematically for women who migrated after the first, second, third, and so on, child. While births were reduced for all categories of women immediately on migration, the earlier in the life cycle that women arrived in Germany, the greater the reduction in fertility. Insofar as giving birth indicates the value of children, movement from Turkish to German society significantly affected this outlook.

A study of 520 Turkish immigrant families to Germany supports this position. Using Turkish families in Turkey and Turks who remigrated from Germany to Turkey as the baseline, Nauck (1988) observed that immigrant mothers showed a rapid change in early child rearing practices that tended toward normative practices of German mothers: 73 percent of the Turkish immigrants said that they took their infants for regular medical checkups, 62 percent said that they fed infants on a schedule, 57 percent followed a medically prescribed diet for their infants, 64 percent allowed their infants to use the entire living space for crawling rather than restrict them to a small area, 50 percent completed toilet training by eighteen months, and infants were breastfed on average for about nine months. These "Germanlike" practices and norms varied directly with years of schooling and time in the family life cycle when migration occurred.

This result is supported by an additional finding on Turkish migrant parents' sex-role concepts. Nauck (1989b) asked about husbands' dominant position in making decisions and about giving boys more schooling than girls. Sex-role norms of Turkish migrants living in Germany differed significantly those of Turkish parents in Turkey, with parents who had migrated to Germany before marriage differing more than parents who migrated later in the family life cycle. Finally, in all categories of migration, mothers more than fathers deviated from traditional norms. Migrating to a new culture influenced parents' views of sex roles, which are integral to family organization and thus imply adaptivity to norms of the host culture. Insofar as early child rearing practices were also altered, we can begin to glimpse the processes that led to a new valuing and definition of childhood.

Findings on sex-role orientation conclude this second series of studies. Nauck (1989a) interviewed 220 Turkish couples about decision making in the home and responsibility for family-related tasks. Five major family types were identified, two of which are relevant here. In the traditional pattern, husbands made major decisions autonomously and took responsibility for major tasks. In the egalitarian pattern, husbands and wives made decisions jointly and shared tasks cooperatively.

Adults in the traditional family pattern showed high reliance on the Turkish infrastructure in Germany for shopping, recreation, and social life. In contrast adults in the more egalitarian pattern showed no less use of the Turkish infrastructure but reported much higher use of German facilities and culture, including those requiring competence in the German language. These data suggest that women may be crucial to the assimilation process and that changes in child rearing practices may be part of a larger restructuring of the woman's role in family organization.

As found with the Croatian immigrants, not all of the Turkish families assimilated, some retained old customs and relied on the ethnic community for daily needs, while others more rapidly ventured out into the host culture. Neither group seemed to give up its ethnic identity, but the latter partook of the host culture more fully. Both types seemed to derive strength from available ethnic resources, but the former relied almost solely on them while the latter partook of both cultures.

Turkish and Croatian immigrants showed individual differences in the degree to which and ways in which they assimilated to the host society. At the same time, these differences were overridden by a shift in child rearing practices and views of children, which approximated the host culture's. For Turkish parents, fertility, early child rearing practices, and sex-role attitudes changed quickly in the direction of German norms. For Croatian parents, the value placed on self-directedness and schooling shifted toward middle-class U.S. norms. As Inkeles (1955) intimated for Russian immigrants to the United

States, Croatian and Turkish immigrants reared their children for the culture they would enter instead of the culture the parents had just left or the culture that the parents preferred for themselves.

What Is Society?

One aim of the present chapter is to encourage psychologists to develop concepts of society that can serve their theoretical interests. The position advanced here is not that of a social determinism in which the sociological macrostructure—for instance, social class membership—defines individuals. Social class does not determine rearing practices; only parents do this by weighing options and making choices based on their knowledge.

What kind of definition of society best serves a psychological position that grants parents cognitive capacities to construct social perspectives? Over the past two decades, a genre of thinking called microsociology has developed to deal with society as a set of face-to-face interactive processes. It assumes that society is composed of patterns of daily interactions, joke telling, conversation, and the like. Rather than being side events, these activities are the means by which persons construct social institutions and establish shared meanings. Macrostructures have existence, but they depend on everyday interactions for their constitution and meaning (Goffman, 1983).

According to this viewpoint, any formal social structure depends on individuals for its maintenance. In a democratic system, for instance, individuals have to act democratically by discussing differences, compromising, letting minorities have a voice, and the like. Such interaction patterns reflect the system, on the one hand, and continuously reconstitute it recursively, on the other hand (Corsaro and Eder, 1990). Hence, structures originate and change through the interactive sphere and their meaning derives from interpersonal exchanges.

This perspective on society seems especially useful for a cognitive psychology grounded on the premise that persons construct reality and that parents construct child rearing practices for the social success of their children (Tesson and Youniss, in press). As Riesman (1953) noted, parents cannot teach what society "is" when society continues to change. What parents can teach are ways in which to participate in interactions, which are the means for constituting and understanding social structures.

Although Baldwin's and Bronfenbrenner's work in the 1950s preceded the birth of microsociology, we can see how their research fits this model. Baldwin proposed that parents within a democratic political system might prefer rearing practices in which misdeeds are discussed and reasoning about them is shared. Bronfenbrenner proposed that in a society that is moving away from scarcity and demanding more education, middle-class parents offer reasons for desired actions rather than simply demand compliance.

The suggestion that studies of parents' cognition take account of sociological factors can now be understood as an attempt to broaden our outlook rather than to reduce it to a sociological perspective. In defining society in terms of microprocesses, the two fields merge on a common interest that involves everyday interactions, of which parent-child exchanges are an essential part. What remains to be studied is how these interactions reflect larger societal structures, how they become parts of children's interactive competence, and how they are modified as children's social contacts expand in the realms of peers, schools, and other domains.

Conclusion

This chapter proposes that parents approach the task of child rearing with sensitivity to the society around them and awareness of the society their children will enter. Parents appear to adopt practices that they think will best serve their children's future social adaptation. We saw that preferred practices (1) change historically (Bronfenbrenner, 1958; Inkeles, 1955; McLoughlin, 1975), (2) differ by social class (Bronfenbrenner, 1958, 1961; Kohn, 1959, 1969; Miller and Sperry, 1987; Nauck, 1989b; Zivkovic, 1990, in press), and (3) are altered as immigrants move from one to another cultural setting (Inkeles, 1955; Nauck, 1987, 1988, 1989a, 1989b; Zivkovic, 1990, in press).

The breadth and coherence of these findings support the initial proposition that psychologists can enrich their theories of child rearing by studying parents' understanding of the society their children will enter. Whether another Rev. Wayland withholds food from his son, or a single, working-class mother in Baltimore toughens her daughter with teasing, parents seem to base their practices on the behavior they think will be useful for their children in particular settings. Hence, parents who migrate to new settings that differ from their home countries alter rearing practices to help their children become better prepared for success in the host society.

It is important that psychologists approach society's role in parents' beliefs with caution. The power of society can too readily support a deterministic argument in which social structure controls the behaviors that are necessary for adaptation. Such a model is not justified by the findings reviewed here, especially the studies on immigration in which parents varied in degree of assimilation and yet appeared to adapt to society. First, variations were found among Croatian immigrants to the United States and Turkish immigrants to Germany in the degree to which individuals followed norms of the host societies. Second, these various levels of assimilation signify alternate ways of adapting to a society. Third, despite these differences, immigrant parents manifested similar rearing practices, which tended toward the dominant mode in the host culture. And, fourth, in many cases, parents held one value system for themselves, while they encouraged their children to adopt the host society.

These findings suggest that individual-society relations are best conceived within a microsociological framework that acknowledges individual and group agency (Tesson and Youniss, in press). This perspective on society fits a cognitive position that is based on the premise that knowledge is constructed by individuals and cooperating groups who reflect on their interactions with one another and social institutions. Knowledge does not pass from a structure to the individual; rather, it is constructed so that individuals and groups can understand and function adaptively in a society.

This view was intimated, for example, by Baldwin's (1955) proposal forty years ago regarding realization of a democratic society through specific parent-child interactions, and by Bronfenbrenner's (1958) understanding of parents' desire to accommodate historical change. We can only imagine how advanced research and theory would be today had this insight been pursued when it was initially offered. With microsociology as a tool, it is even more intriguing to imagine the advances that can come in the future.

References

Baldwin, A. L. *Behavior and Development in Childhood.* New York: Dryden, 1955.

Becker, W. "Parent Discipline." In M. L. Hoffman and L. W. Hoffman (eds.), *Review of Child Development Research.* Vol. 1. New York: Russell Sage Foundation, 1964.

Bronfenbrenner, U. "Socialization and Social Class Through Time and Space." In E. E. Maccoby, T. M. Newcomb, and E. L. Hartley (eds.), *Readings in Social Psychology.* Troy, Mo.: Holt, Rinehart & Winston, 1958.

Bronfenbrenner, U. "The Changing American Child: A Speculative Analysis." *Journal of Social Issues,* 1961, *17* (1), 6–18.

Corsaro, W. A., and Eder, D. "Children's Peer Cultures." *Annual Review of Sociology,* 1990, *16,* 197–220.

Gadlin, H. "Child Discipline and the Pursuit of Self." In H. W. Reese and L. Lipsitt (eds.), *Advances in Child Development and Behavior.* Vol. 13. San Diego: Academic Press, 1978.

Goffman, E. "The Interaction Order." *American Sociological Review,* 1983, *48* (1), 1–17.

Goodnow, J. J. "Parents' Ideas, Actions, and Feelings: Models and Methods from Developmental and Social Psychology." *Child Development,* 1988, *59* (2), 286–320.

Hoffman, M. L. "Moral Development." In P. H. Mussen (ed.), *Carmichael's Manual of Child Psychology.* New York: Wiley, 1970.

Inkeles, A. "Social Change and Social Character: The Role of Parental Mediation." *Journal of Social Issues,* 1955, *11* (1), 12–23.

Kohlberg, L. "Stage and Sequence: A Cognitive-Developmental Approach to Socialization." In D. A. Goslin (ed.), *Handbook of Socialization Theory and Research.* Skokie, Ill.: Rand McNally, 1969.

Kohn, M. L. "Social Class and the Exercise of Parental Authority." *American Sociological Review,* 1959, *24* (3), 352–366.

Kohn, M. L. *Class and Conformity: A Study of Values.* Belmont, Calif.: Dorsey Press, 1969.

Kuczynski, L. "Socialization Goals and Mother-Child Interaction: Strategies for Long-Term and Short-Term Compliance." *Developmental Psychology,* 1984, *20* (6), 1061–1073.

McGillicuddy-DeLisi, A. V. "Parental Beliefs About Developmental Processes." *Human Development,* 1982, *25* (3), 192–200.

McLoughlin, W. G. "Evangelical Childrearing in the Age of Jackson." *Journal of Social History,* 1975, *9* (1), 20–39.

Miller, D. R., and Swanson, G. E. *Inner Conflict and Defense.* Troy, Mo.: Holt, Rinehart & Winston, 1960.

Miller, P. J., and Sperry, L. L. "The Socialization of Anger and Aggression." *Merrill-Palmer Quarterly,* 1987, *33* (1), 1–31.

Moos, R. H., and Moos, B. S. *Manual for the Family Environment Scale.* Palo Alto, Calif.: Consulting Psychologists Press, 1981.

Nauck, B. "Migration and Reproductive Behavior in Turkish Migrant Families." In C. Kagitcibasi (ed.), *Growth and Progress in Cross-Cultural Psychology*. Berwyn, Pa.: Swets, 1987.

Nauck, B. "Migration and Change in Parent-Child Relationships." *International Migration,* 1988, *26* (1), 33–56.

Nauck, B. "Assimilation Process and Group Integration of Migrant Families." *International Migration,* 1989a, 27 (1), 27–48.

Nauck, B. "Intergenerational Relationships in Families from Turkey and Germany." *European Sociological Review,* 1989b, *5* (3), 251–274.

Riesman, D. *The Lonely Crowd.* New York: Doubleday, 1953.

Sigel, I. E. (ed.). *Parental Belief Systems: The Psychological Consequences for Children.* Hillsdale, N.J.: Erlbaum, 1985.

Tesson, G., and Youniss, J. "A Theory of Psychological Development for Micro Sociology." In A. M. Ambert (ed.), *Sociological Studies of Children.* Greenwich, Conn.: JAI Press, in press.

Wertsch, J. V., and Youniss, J. "Contextualizing the Investigator: The Case of Developmental Psychology." *Human Development,* 1987, *30* (1), 18–31.

Whiting, B. *Six Cultures.* New York: Wiley, 1963.

Zivkovic, I. "Strategies Used by Croatian Parents to Influence Their Adolescents' Behavior." *Journal of Croatian Studies,* 1990, *30* (1), 3–50.

Zivkovic, I. "Adaptation Patterns of Parents and Their Children in the U.S. and Canada." In M. Hofer, P. Noack, and J. Youniss (eds.), *Psychological Responses to Social Change.* Berlin: Mouton de Gruyter, in press.

JAMES YOUNISS is professor of psychology and director of the Life Cycle Institute at Catholic University of America, Washington, D.C.

A lack of agreement between generations need not be regarded as dysfunctional or as a source for parental action. An alternative analysis directs attention to when parents care about a lack of agreement, suggests several ways in which a lack of agreement may come about, and prompts a variety of new research questions.

Acceptable Disagreement Across Generations

Jacqueline J. Goodnow

One of the benefits of asking about the social-cognitive aspects of parenting is that it encourages a fresh look at long-standing issues. The issue taken up in this chapter has to do with the extent to which parents and children hold the same views of events: the same values, the same goals, the same ways of interpreting a child's or a parent's behavior. That topic is usually presented under the labels of intergenerational agreement, congruence, disagreement, or conflict. It is the underlying topic also in discussions of the internalization of parental values and in some analyses of compliance and noncompliance.

The new directions proposed here are threefold. In essence, they consist of taking a different look at outcomes, processes, and the family framework within which the topic is set. My concern with the way we usually view outcomes is to a large extent signaled by part of this chapter's title: "acceptable disagreement." It is easy to assume that "the good outcome"—from a parent's or a clinician's viewpoint—is a match across generations, with the term *match* implying similarity. *Disagreement* or *difference,* then, has the connotation of conflict or of unsuccessful socialization. Accompanying this assumption is often the expectation that a discrepancy, once a parent or child is aware of it, will lead to action. Some move will be made to reduce the gap. Parents, for instance, will reconsider their position or attempt to change the child's view. Rather than make these assumptions, I instead ask, Why regard agreement as the only good outcome, or as an outcome of importance to parents? When do parents care about differences? When do they regard a difference as unimportant, tolerable, acceptable, or even pleasing?

Asking when parents care prompts the second new direction: a closer look at processes. The emphasis in cross-generation studies is usually on whether or not a particular outcome—congruence—occurs. How this comes about has been given a lesser degree of attention. When we ask about when parents care, however, processes begin to demand a greater degree of attention. We can then begin to ask, for example, about the ways in which parents signal the significance of a message or the presence of alternatives to acceptance. We also can begin to ask about the extent to which the child cares: about the child's interest in being alert to a parent's message, in locating alternatives to acceptance, in exploring the possibilities and limits of resistance, and in learning the acceptable styles of resisting or of negotiating an alternative.

The third and last new direction has to do with the framework within which we place the analysis of parents' ideas. I have in the past argued for the value of making two links. One is to general analyses of cognition: social cognition or "classic" cognition (for example, Goodnow, 1988). The other is to analyses of what have been called "social representations" (Carugati, 1990; von Cranach, Doise, and Mugny, 1992) or "cultural models" (D'Andrade and Strauss, 1992; Goodnow and Collins, 1990). This second kind of approach to cognition—the analysis of ideas as social representations or cultural models— is probably the less familiar to developmental psychologists. I draw particular attention to it, however, because one of its central concerns has to do with the nature and sources of shared and unshared meanings within a social or a cultural group. The referent group is now larger than that of the family. Bringing together the lines of interest in sharing meanings that are family-based or culture-based, however, should benefit both.

This third direction (developing frameworks) figures predominantly in the first section of this chapter (a brief statement about the background of my interest in acceptable disagreement). The other directions (asking when parents care about a difference and taking a second look at the processes that result in agreement or divergence) are taken up in later sections. The final comments then deal with a research direction implicit in the earlier sections, namely, the need to give renewed attention to parents' goals.

Background

My interest in cross-generation agreement had its real beginning in Judith Cashmore's proposal of the topic for her Ph.D. thesis. Her study asked about conditions influencing the extent to which Australian adolescents and their parents (immigrant or native-born) held the same ideas about occupational goals, routes to success, and the importance of characteristics such as being neat, obedient, curious, or considerate of others. That study led to the proposal that the analysis of convergent and divergent views across generations needed to consider two steps: (1) the child's perception of the message (this could be accurate or inaccurate) and (2) the child's acceptance or rejection of the perceived message. A lack of match could stem from either step: from inaccurate perception or from rejection. Each step was also likely to be influenced by different conditions. The clarity of a parent's message, for instance, was most likely to influence the first step—perception. The warmth of a relationship was most likely to influence the second—acceptance or rejection (Cashmore and Goodnow, 1985).

Some of the additions to that model were prompted by my writing a review of issues of cross-generation divergence (Goodnow, 1992). Others were prompted by my work with Joan Grusec on methods of discipline in relation to aspects of internalization (Grusec and Goodnow, 1994), and by recent reconceptualizations of compliance and family conflict. Smetana (1988a, 1988b), for instance, asked when a disagreement about who should make the rules for a child results in a conflict, and she linked cases of disagreement without conflict to the sophistication of a child's argument. Kuczynski and Kochanska (1990) asked, Is noncompliance always dysfunctional? When is it a source of concern to parents? When is it regarded in more accepting or positive terms, treated as part of encouraging children to develop acceptable ways of negotiating, of expressing autonomy?

That type of questioning fit nicely with my own concerns. I had for some time held the view that there were some aspects of child development that adults cared about and some they did not, and that psychologists who concentrated on different aspects were led to different theories about development. Few parents, for instance, are concerned about whether or not children acquire an understanding of conservation in the Piagetian sense. Most of the variance in children's understanding, then, can be attributed to factors within the child. For these topics, standard Piagetian theory works very well.

In contrast, most parents are concerned about a child's understanding of what it means to be honest, fair, or respectful. The child is under pressure to come into some degree of agreement with the views held by the parent. For these topics, it is not reasonable to think of children as constructing their views of the world in happy isolation from others. A different kind of theory needs to come into play (Goodnow, Knight, and Cashmore, 1985). Nor is it reasonable to think of parents as caring equally about every area in which they do take an interest. To assume this equivalence would be to repeat the difficulty that D'Andrade (1981) pointed to within research by cognitive psychologists. In the course of treating every cognitive problem as equivalent to every other kind of problem, he noted, we have lost sight of the fact that some forms of competence are insisted upon, that is, we must acquire these in order to be regarded as members of our social group, whereas others are optional. If we extend D'Andrade's insight to analyses of parent-child agreement, the question quickly arises, When and how do parents highlight some messages as more important than others?

Supplementing this line of my concern was an approach to parents' ideas that starts from a different view of agreement and that draws attention to the need to analyze the processes by which agreement comes about. In essence, this approach first proposes that differences and divergences might be considered as the norm: All social groups contain a variety of viewpoints, coexisting or competing. Adults move toward greater agreement with some views rather than others, however, when these views become part of their daily practices (they take on employment, for instance, as day-care staff [Emiliani, Zani, and Carugati, 1981]) or part of their identities (people become, for instance, parents or teachers [Carugati, 1990]). In effect, agreement occurs only under some conditions and consists of some selective appropriation from the viewpoints available. The argument has been stated in terms of the views held by adults, but it is clearly extendable to children and to their agreements with parents' views. At the least, one is led to ask, Where does selectivity appear in a child's acceptance or rejection of a parent's message? And how does such selectivity come about?

These several points have raised two related questions. When do parents care about similarity or difference? What kind of model does one now need to have for the ways in which agreement or divergence comes about?

When Do Parents Care?

This question is also raised by Grusec, Hastings, and Mammone (this volume, Chapter One) and by Smetana (this volume, Chapter Two). Grusec, Dix, and Mills (1982) raised some time ago, for instance, the question of why parents are more upset by a child's antisocial acts than by a child's failure to be prosocial. I anchor the question in a particular moment for a parent. He or she has become aware that a child holds a position that is different from that held by the parent. Two questions are possible: When is a parent concerned? When does a parent, or a child, take action to reduce the gap? The two questions are not identical, and the two states—feeling concerned and taking action—are likely to reflect different conditions. The first state, feeling concerned, is also likely to be a prerequisite for the second, along with a sense that taking action to reduce the gap may make a difference. I concentrate on the first question: When is a difference a source of concern? My suggested answers are the following:

When the parent has some investment in similarity. To be concerned, a parent must first have some wish for similarity, some degree of interest in reproduction or continuity. Parents, I propose do *not* always hope for this. I may, in fact, hope that my children will adopt goals that were not mine, will see the world in ways that I did not, will go beyond me.

When the parent's position allows for little "value" stretch. I take the term *value stretch* from Rodman (1963), who used it as a way of differentiating among parents. Some parents, he argued, can stretch their positions easily. They can, for instance, deescalate the wish that a child would become a professional—a physician, a lawyer, and so on—to the wish that the child would have a "decent" job, a "clean" job, or "some job." Others, Rodman argued, can tolerate less stretch. They are then the more likely to be stung into action. Rodman's comment was with reference to differences in socioeconomic status, but the concept of differences in stretch can be extended beyond this comparison.

When the difference is not a difference between tolerable alternatives but instead extends beyond the parent's bottom line. The child's position, to pick up the notion of stretch again, is now beyond what the parent's position or expectation can stretch to. This form of difference may be particularly relevant at adolescence. Adolescents, to quote a friend who is also a parent, have "an unerring instinct for the jugular": a statement that points to the adolescents' active steps not toward disguising a difference but toward making one visible and toward the choice of a content area where the parent will definitely feel concern.

When the difference is not softened by the way the child disagrees or by the saving attributions that a parent may make. This general heading covers several possibilities: (1) The difference is not accompanied by acceptable ways of expressing a difference. That condition is suggested by results from Kuczynski and Kochanska's (1990) study of noncompliance among young children and by Smetana's (1988a, 1988b) study of parent-child disagreement. (2) The difference in one area cannot be offset by finding a positive in some other area. A concrete example of mitigated difference comes from a mother describing a seven-year-old son: "He's hopeless as far as his room goes, but he'll do anything with his father outside, so I'll settle for that for now." Parents use this mitigating tactic with any expectation and at all ages: "He's not talking yet," said the mother of a sixteen-month-old, "but he walks very well." (3) The difference cannot be offset by a saving attribution. I have in mind, for instance, data indicating that parents become more upset by children's transgressions as children become older (Dix, Ruble, Grusec, and Nixon, 1986). Then it is no longer easy to write off a difference by regarding it as "a passing phase" or "something they'll grow out of."

When the difference implies a general problem extending beyond this particular difference. Let me suggest two such possibilities: (1) The difference implies that the parent has been unsuccessful. This is likely to be a special source of concern when the parent sees himself or herself as having made a sizable effort (that is, one is denied the attribution that perhaps a little more effort would have changed the course of events). This implication, of course, contains the assumption that the way in which a child turns out is a reflection of the parents' work, rather than a reflection of either the child's "good" or "bad" genes or some unhappy circumstances. A particular level of upset, I might add, may be expected when the implication that the parent is doing a poor job is public. (2) The difference implies that the relationship is in trouble. An example is Loevinger's (1959) argument that the essence of a generation gap is when a child imputes to a parent a motive that is the opposite—the negative opposite—of the image the parent is trying to convey. The parent, for instance, inhibits the impulse to anger or retaliation and proceeds to talk calmly and rationally about the problem. The child, however, perceives this action as punitive, as "talking me to death." Worse still, the child may see this action as something that the parent "always" does, as a sign of the parent's generally negative attitude or generally negative intentions. This implication rarely sits well with parents' images of themselves and of their relationship with a child. The parent's image, however, is not all that is at stake. All areas of interaction, all attempts at influence or even of mutual good feeling, are now at risk, likely to be always interpreted as a sign of a parent's "meanness" or "indifference." Proof to the contrary—proof that will be seen as convincing—may now be hard to supply.

Steps on the Way to Agreement or Difference

The previous section focused on the last point of a sequence: A parent notices a lack of agreement, a difference in opinion. Before this point is reached, however, a number of previous steps must occur, steps that should bring out the several processes involved along the way to the end of an interaction cycle.

To bring out those steps, I focus now on the start of a sequence rather than on the end point (noticing a difference). The proposal expands on the two-part sequence discussed in Cashmore and Goodnow (1985). In the revised sequence, there are four steps: (1) The parent expresses a position or conveys a message, (2) the child notices and interprets (accurately or inaccurately), (3) the child accepts or rejects, and (4) some follow-up action occurs (the parent, for instance, notices the divergence and acts to reduce the difference in opinion, perhaps by starting a new cycle again, restating his or her position). I consider each step in turn and, for each step, highlight questions that need to be asked, directions that we might follow.

Parent Expresses a Position, Conveys a Message. Two questions stand out: How is a position expressed (and what gives rise to the choice of one means rather than another)? What is the nature of the parent's position? Rather than a position that is pro or con, I propose that parents are often indicating a range of alternatives: some optimal, some tolerable, and some "out of the question."

Ways of Expressing a Position. Parents often use indirect statements when talking to children (Becker and Goodnow, 1992). For example, parents ask, "Were you born in a barn?" when they want a child to close the door. They ask, "What's the magic word?" when they want the child to say please or thank you. Parents also say, "I'm not running a taxi service," "This is not a hotel, boarding house, restaurant, delicatessen, laundromat," or "The maid didn't come today": indirect ways of signaling to a child that an expectation or a request is inappropriate (that is at least one of the implicit messages).

Perhaps because psychologists have been especially concerned with the benefits of offering children explicit reasons for good behaviors, indirect approaches have received relatively little attention. They deserve more, both because of their frequency (in Becker's [1988] analysis of conversations between parents and preschool children, indirect statements represented 80 to 90 percent of parents' statements about polite talk) and because they force us to ask, Why are parents not acting as psychological studies suggest that they should? That is, why are parents not offering explicit rationales for doing the right thing? The answer, Becker and I suspect, has to do with the history of interactions. Explicit rationales are probably offered most often at the start of a child's induction into correct behavior. The indirect statements then come at a time when the child has had, in the parent's eyes, ample exposure to the message. Now the task is one of disrupting routine inattention to what the parent has said and of having the child take over some of the work of remembering and reflecting, starting with the question "What is this strange statement about?"

Another finding underlines again the need to consider how parents state their positions. This was mothers' use of drama, of theater. The sample respondents whom my colleagues and I interviewed in Sydney for reports on household work and interactions related to it were Anglo in origin. Drama is not supposed to be part of their stock-in-trade. That is supposed to belong to the people often referred to by the Anglos in Australia as "Mediterranean." Nonetheless, our Anglo mothers often described themselves as "having a rant and a rave," "going into my fishwife act," "chucking one of my mentals" (Goodnow and Delaney, 1989; Goodnow and Warton, 1991). What purposes does such theater serve? And how do children interpret it? One purpose must be to underline not so much the content of the parent's message as its significance. The message goes well beyond whether a parent holds a particular viewpoint or not. In effect, the parent is now signaling that this is something he or she really cares about.

Nature of the Parent's Message. We tend easily to think of parents' messages in terms of their referential content: "I am a liberal," for instance, or "I would like you to follow in my footsteps, marry within our religious group," and so on. We need, however, to consider any message as also containing some marker of its significance to a parent. We also need to think of any message as indicating the degree of negotiability that is possible.

My interest in this aspect of a message was initially sparked by the frequency with which Australian mothers remarked, to interviewers and to children, that some behaviors were "not on," a phrase indicating that some theoretically possible ways of acting or thinking should be completely ruled out. When asked, for instance, if a child could pay a brother or sister to do the child's household tasks, the swift and firm answer from most of our sample Australian mothers was "Oh no, that's not on." For this possibility, there were no shades of gray, no room for negotiation.

This kind of statement, I propose, is not an isolated phenomenon. More broadly, parents appear to regularly convey to their children the presence or absence of a range of alternatives. They indicate to their children what will be optimal, what will be tolerable, what is "close to the bottom line," and what is "beyond the pale," completely unacceptable. When it comes to children's household jobs, for instance, the ideal may well be a situation in which children volunteer their labor, cheerfully and as a gift, an act of love. In the tolerable range are acts of work done with varying incentives or varying degrees of pressure. Beyond the tolerable range—at least around the ages of ten to fourteen years—are situations where work is done only for money, or on a piecework basis: specific amounts for specific jobs (Goodnow and Warton, 1991; Warton and Goodnow, in press).

Why propose the range of alternatives as a direction for particular attention in the future? The reasons are several. One is that this way of looking at interactions may be widely useful. It is, for instance, in line with a proposal from Valsiner (1984). In the course of watching mothers feed their two-year-olds, Valsiner noted that mothers responded to their children's actions in several ways. Some actions they encouraged. Some they tolerated. A second reason is that the knowledge of possible alternatives—of limits, of shades of acceptability—may be the critical part of what children acquire. It even seems possible that what is learned first is the parent's limit, the bottom line. A third reason is that children may be particularly interested in learning the range, in knowing where the limits are and what alternatives a parent will consider or settle for. A fourth, and last, is that differences between parents and children may be thought of as being about the place of a particular viewpoint or action within the spectrum, with affect becoming most marked when parent and child approach each other's bottom line, each other's non-negotiable sticking point.

Child Notices and Interprets. A necessary part of any new direction is increased attention to what the child comes to understand as the parent's viewpoint, with particular attention to the understanding of significance and of the range of alternatives. We might well ask, for instance, what children see their parents as settling for or as placing in the non-negotiable basket.

Less obviously, we need also to consider more fully the child's part in monitoring for a parent's viewpoint or preferences. We tend to study agreement (or compliance) very much from the parent's point of view. In many ways, our working model appears to be one of an observant, listening child, in need only of a parent who makes clear what is needed and why. The reality, at least in many of our studies of children's contributions to the work of a household, seems closer to a "deaf" child, with the parent then feeling forced to play the role of nagger, broken record, or producer of innovative ways (mysteriously indirect statements and drama probably play a role here) to gain and keep the child's attention (Goodnow and Delaney, 1989; Goodnow and Warton, 1991). At the least, we need to ask not only about the conditions under which an attentive child is accurate in his or her perception of a parent's message but also about the circumstances under which the child puts more or less attention into being alert to where a parent stands on an issue.

To turn these general proposals into a specific research question, we might start from the child's need to interpret not only what a parent says but also the way in which the message is delivered. Suppose the parent in this case has made use of drama, of theater. How do children interpret this behavior? How do they come to recognize that this is theater, to know that the situation is serious enough to warrant taking cover for a while, but that the anger and the upset will "blow themselves out"? To use the description of one mother, the children "tiptoe for a while" but they also say to one another, "There she goes again." Presumably, the mother indicates in some way that her words do not have face value, that her actions only seem out of control. The nature of these cues, however, and the ways in which they are picked up and interpreted by children, are as yet unknowns.

Child Accepts or Rejects the Perceived Message. Questions about the degree of agreement are always a part of studies of congruence across generations. We ask, for instance, whether adolescents attach the same degree of importance to being neat or obedient as they see their parents assigning (Cashmore and Goodnow, 1985). Or we ask adults who are staking out new territory (dividing work on nongendered lines or becoming political activists) whether they see their actions and viewpoints as extending or sharply departing from the ways and views of their parents (see Goodnow and Bowes, 1994, for household divisions; Block, 1972, for political activism).

What needs to be explored if we are to increase our understanding of this step and of the processes behind it? One critical move consists of asking, What part of the parental message is accepted or rejected? In the case of the political activists, for instance, there is divergence when it comes to radical acts of protest (divergence in the sense that parents did not act in this way). There appears, however, to be convergence and acceptance of what might be regarded as a higher-order message: "Whatever you do, be committed; don't be apathetic or half-hearted."

A second needed move is attention to the question What particular conditions promote acceptance or rejection? The two main proposals in the literature are for an impact from self-interest (each generation's stake, for instance, in similarity or difference; Bengston and Kuypers, 1971) and from the warmth of the relationship (Furstenburg, 1971; Cashmore and Goodnow, 1985). Neither of these proposals has been adequately checked for specific effects on accurate perception or on acceptance of the perceived message. The effects of warmth, for instance, remain in the state that Furstenburg (1971) drew attention to some time ago: explored in connection with the final measure of convergence or divergence, but not with regard to the steps along the way to that point.

The third and last move to be noted arises from work by Smetana (1988a, 1988b) and by Kuczynski and Kochanska (1990). It has to do with the style of acceptance or rejection. We know intuitively that acceptance in the form of "if you say so" can often be less than what a parent seeks. Nonetheless, styles of acceptance have attracted little research attention. Styles of rejection are beginning to attract more notice. Smetana (1988a, 1988b), for instance, emphasized the importance of the level of sophistication with which an adolescent expresses his or her views on what should set the rules or make decisions about friends, music, the state of one's room, or the hours one keeps. Disagreement accompanied by a sophisticated argument (a level of argument that presumably is approved of by parents or that is like their own) causes less sense of conflict than when disagreement is expressed with less elegance. In similar fashion, preschoolers who reject their parents' wishes with a defiant "no" cause parents more concern than do those who offer to "do it later" or who offer a reason for not going along with a directive (Kuczynski and Kochanska, 1990).

We now need to ask, Why does style matter so much? And what styles are optimal, tolerable, or completely unacceptable? One specific possibility, prompted by considering the position of immigrant parents, is that a child may disagree with a parent in a way that implies some respect for the parent's position, some need to take it into account. The two may then argue, or agree to disagree, but each person acknowledges that the other has something to say and understands what is said. That style of divergence seems less likely to be disturbing than a style that implies that one person's viewpoint holds no meaning for the other. The parent's viewpoint is, for instance, written off from the start as "one of those ideas from the old country." The lack of consideration may not even be so active. The parent's position may simply be so much the product of a particular period, a particular history, that although the words are understood, none of the real meaning is grasped. Those are different routes to nonacceptance: routes with different meanings to the parent (or to the child, whose views may also be written off or seem to have no real meaning for parents even when parents are trying to understand).

Divergence Is Noticed and Responded To. Studies of congruence across generations usually stop at the point of asking whether the two sets of viewpoints are similar to or different from each other. Developmentalists, however, will surely need to ask a further question: What happens after a state of convergence or divergence—the latter especially—has arisen? This point is, for instance, a concern of Collins and Luebker (this volume, Chapter Five).

An earlier section of this chapter focuses on one part of this step: When are parents upset or disturbed by the presence of difference? I concentrate now on a different aspect of responding to divergence. This is the assumption that parents will be aware of a difference between the way they view the world and the way their children do. That assumption may well hold for studies of noncompliance, where parents are aware that they have issued a directive or made a request, and that the child had either done nothing, said no, or begun some process of bargaining ("later," "looks okay to me," "all my friends," "why me?" and so on).

Awareness of a difference, however, is definitely not to be taken for granted. To take a personal example, I am only now discovering a number of differences between the views held by my children, when they were adolescents, and the views held by their parents. This late discovery is not for lack of interest on my part. Instead, the contributing factor appears to be more in the form of active steps by the younger generation: their wish to disguise or soften a difference, both to give themselves undisturbed time to work out what they thought and to prevent their parents from becoming worried. The active, *visible* steps that children take to avoid divergence strike me as a topic in need of exploration. It is not simply that we know little about these steps. More broadly, an exploration of how children disguise or soften differences can provide a specific way to start considering children's contributions to the area of convergence and divergence. Parents are not the only parties involved, and their being taken by surprise by a divergence may not always represent their lack of concern or of monitoring.

A Last Research Direction

I have already pointed to a number of gaps in what we know about the cognitive aspects of parenting. In this final section, I focus on the need for further analyses of goals and intentions.

Why select parents' goals and intentions as a particular focus? One reason is that we seem unlikely to increase our understanding of when parents notice divergence, are concerned about its occurrence, or take any action unless we know more about parents' goals. The course of any interaction is likely to be different when a parent seeks not short-term agreement or compliance but a child's acquisition of acceptable ways of saying no (Kuczynski and Kochanska, 1990), or the development and maintenance of a comfortable relationship with the child (Grusec and Goodnow, 1994).

A second reason is that, without an analysis of goals, we are unlikely even to know what a parent counts as agreement or disagreement. As a parent, I may count it as agreement if my child and I both hold a common view of the bottom line, ignoring all the rest. As a parent, I may also aim at a particular level of understanding. I may expect, for instance, that the child agrees with what Wertheim (1975) called a "ground rule": a rule at the level of "Don't leave your dirty clothes on the floor." Or I may expect that the child hears and accepts a metarule such as "Don't expect other people to pick up after you." Moreover, those levels of understanding may shift with age. The older the child, the more likely it seems that parents will hope for an understanding of metarules (for what Mancuso and Lehrer [1986] call the "implicative structure" of statements) and will be disappointed if only the ground rule is understood or if the child, to take a phrase from T. S. Eliot, does "the right thing for the wrong reason."

If we turn the research spotlight on goals and intentions, what directions might we pursue? At the least, we need to ask, How do goals differ from one another, and which particular goals are especially relevant to the issue of agreement or divergence? I have already noted two possible distinctions among goals: one between short-term and long-term goals (Kuczynski and Kochanska, 1990) and the other related to the level of agreement that is sought (Wertheim, 1975). Dix (1991, 1992) contributed a third, distinguishing between goals that reflect parents' concerns for themselves (a concern, for example, with getting a certain amount of work done or achieving some quiet time) and goals that reflect the child's concerns, as perceived by the parent. Bargh and Gollwitzer (in press), writing within the framework of classical cognitive studies, distinguished between goals that have an implementation tag attached to them (for example, "I shall do this next Thursday on my way to work") and goals that do not. Bargh (1990) distinguished also between goals that lead to proactive behaviors ("I do this in order to achieve a goal") and those that lead to reactive behaviors ("I act when I perceive a violation").

For analyses of correspondence between generations, those several distinctions are all useful. So also there should be attention to a further goal, one that we can call "establishing a bias in interpretations." It is unlikely that parents and children proceed only by carefully appraising each specific event, each specific occasion of a similarity or a divergence, as it appears. Our general sense of whether the other means well or has our welfare at heart must create a bias in those appraisals, and this perhaps shortcuts any process of appraisal. The ultimate parental goal, and a major part of what one means by a "good relationship" or "receptive compliance" (Maccoby, 1984), may be that of creating a climate in which interpretations contain a bias. The bias one seeks should make it easier for the child to separate a specific difference of opinion from the general issue of goodwill or caring. The bias one seeks should also make it more, rather than less, likely that a child will see a parental action—however painful it may appear—as "for the child's own good." How children come to perceive a general climate of intentions, how a parent creates a general climate of goodwill and genuine interest, and what the signs are that children use to perceive goodwill are critical research issues for the study of correspondence and of parenting in general.

Have I then ended with a link only to frameworks drawn from conventional studies of cognition? I began by saying that the analysis of parents' ideas needs to be linked to two kinds of approaches to cognition: the type of approach offered by cognitive psychologists for "classic" or social cognition and the type of approach offered by social psychologists and anthropologists under the heading of social representations or cultural models. If I end with an emphasis on implementation goals or biases in interpretation, it may seem that the latter type of approach has been honored only in passing. That impression would be misleading. A concern with socially shared ideas is an equally necessary base for considering distinctions among goals. There is a difference, for instance, between goals that a parent is likely to find endorsed by others in the social group and goals that are not reinforced, supported, or echoed by others outside the family. In addition, it is unlikely that biases in a child's interpretation are the work only of what a parent does. Any bias is also built on the group's position as to what to do or think in cases of doubt. "Parents are wise and experienced" reflects a very different cultural bias from that of "Trust no one over thirty." In short, both approaches need to be kept in mind and drawn on if we are to move toward the development of effective social-cognitive models of convergence and divergence across generations, or of parenting in general.

References

Bargh, J. A. "Auto-Motives: Preconscious Determinants of Social Interaction." In R. M. Sorrentino and E. T. Higgins (eds.), *Handbook of Motivation and Cognition*. Hillsdale, N.J.: Erlbaum, 1990.

Bargh, J. A., and Gollwitzer, P. M. "Environmental Control of Goal-Directed Action: Automatic and Strategic Contingencies Between Situations and Behavior." *Nebraska Symposium on Motivation, 1993.* Lincoln: University of Nebraska Press, in press.

Becker, J. A. "The Success of Parents' Indirect Techniques for Teaching Their Preschoolers Pragmatic Skills." *First Language,* 1988, *8,* 173–182.

Becker, J. A., and Goodnow, J. J. " 'What's the Magic Word?' 'Were You Born in a Tent?' The Challenge of Accounting for Parents' Indirect Use of Speech with Children." *Newsletter of the Laboratory of Comparative Human Development,* 1992, *50* (3), 517–522.

Bengston, V. L., and Kuypers, J. A. "Generational Difference and the Development Stake." *Aging and Human Development,* 1971, *2* (2), 249–260.

Block, J. "Generational Continuity and Discontinuity in the Understanding of Societal Rejection." *Journal of Personality and Social Psychology,* 1972, *22* (2), 333–345.

Carugati, F. F. "Everyday Ideas, Theoretical Models, and Social Representations: The Case of Intelligence and Its Development." In G. R. Semin and K. J. Gergen (eds.), *Everyday Understanding: Social and Scientific Implications.* Newbury Park, Calif.: Sage, 1990.

Cashmore, J., and Goodnow, J. J. "Agreement Between Generations: A Two-Process Model." *Child Development,* 1985, *56* (3), 493–501.

D'Andrade, R. G. "The Cultural Part of Cognition." *Cognitive Science,* 1981, *5,* 179–195.

D'Andrade, R. G., and Strauss, C. *Human Motives and Cultural Models.* New York: Cambridge University Press, 1992.

Dix, T. H. "The Affective Organization of Parenting: Adaptive and Maladaptive Processes." *Psychological Bulletin,* 1991, *110* (1), 3–25.

Dix, T. H. "Parenting on Behalf of the Child: Empathic Goals in the Regulation of Responsive Parenting." In I. E. Sigel, A. V. McGillicuddy-DeLisi, and J. J. Goodnow (eds.), *Parental Belief Systems: The Psychological Consequences for Children.* (2nd ed.) Hillsdale, N.J.: Erlbaum, 1992.

Dix, T. H., Ruble, D. N., Grusec, J. E., and Nixon, S. "Social Cognition in Parents: Inferential and Affective Reactions to Children of Three Age Levels." *Child Development,* 1986, *57* (4), 879–894.

Emiliani, F., Zani, B., and Carugati, F. "From Staff Interactions to the Social Representations of Adults in a Day Nursery." In W. P. Robinson (ed.), *Communication in Development.* San Diego: Academic Press, 1981.

Furstenburg, F. F. "The Transmission of Mobility Orientation in the Family." *Social Forces,* 1971, *49,* 595–603.

Goodnow, J. J. "Parents' Ideas, Actions, and Feelings: Models and Methods from Developmental and Social Psychology." *Child Development,* 1988, *59* (2), 286–320.

Goodnow, J. J. "Parents' Ideas and Children's Ideas: Bases of Congruence and Divergence." In J. E. Sigel, A. V. McGillicuddy-DeLisi, and J. J. Goodnow (eds.), *Parental Belief Systems: The Psychological Consequences for Children.* (2nd ed.) Hillsdale, N.J.: Erlbaum, 1992.

Goodnow, J. J., and Bowes, J. M. *Men, Women, and Household Work: Couples Illustrating Change.* New York: Oxford University Press, 1994.

Goodnow, J. J., and Collins, W. A. *Development According to Parents: The Nature, Sources, and Consequences of Parents' Ideas.* Hillsdale, N.J.: Erlbaum, 1990.

Goodnow, J. J., and Delaney, S. "Children's Household Work: Differentiating Types of Work and Styles of Assignment." *Journal of Applied Developmental Psychology,* 1989, *10* (2), 209–226.

Goodnow, J. J., Knight, R., and Cashmore, J. "Adult Social Cognition: Implications of Parents' Ideas for Approaches to Development." In M. Perlmutter (ed.), *Social Cognition.* Minnesota Symposia on Child Development, vol. 18. Hillsdale, N.J.: Erlbaum, 1985.

Goodnow, J. J., and Warton, P. M. "The Social Bases of Social Cognition: Interactions About Household Work and Their Implications." *Merrill-Palmer Quarterly,* 1991, *37* (1), 27–58.

Grusec, J. E., Dix, T., and Mills, R. "The Effects of Type, Severity, and Victim of Children's Transgressions on Maternal Discipline." *Canadian Journal of Behavioural Science,* 1982, *14* (4), 276–289.

Grusec, J. E., and Goodnow, J. J. "The Impact of Parental Discipline Methods on the Child's

Internalization of Values: A Reconceptualization of Current Points of View." *Developmental Psychology,* 1994, *30* (1), 4–19.

Kuczynski, L., and Kochanska, G. "The Development of Children's Non-Compliance Strategies from Toddlerhood to Age Five." *Developmental Psychology,* 1990, *26* (3), 398–408.

Loevinger, J. "Patterns of Parenthood as Theories of Learning." *Journal of Abnormal and Social Psychology,* 1959, *59,* 148–150.

Maccoby, E. E. "Socialization and Developmental Change." *Child Development,* 1984, *55* (2), 317–328.

Mancuso, J. C., and Lehrer, R. "Cognitive Processes During Reactions to Rule Violation." In R. D. Ashmore and D. M. Brodzinsky (eds.), *Thinking About the Family: Views of Parents and Children.* Hillsdale, N.J.: Erlbaum, 1986.

Rodman, H. "The Lower-Class Value Stretch." *Social Forces,* 1963, *42,* 205–215.

Smetana, J. G. "Adolescents' and Parents' Conceptions of Parental Authority." *Child Development,* 1988a, *59* (2), 321–335.

Smetana, J. G. "Concepts of Self and Social Convention: Adolescents' and Parents' Reasoning About Hypothetical and Actual Family Conflicts." In M. Gunnar and W. A. Collins (eds.), *Development During the Transition to Adolescence.* Minnesota Symposia on Child Development, vol. 21. Hillsdale, N.J.: Erlbaum, 1988b.

Valsiner, J. "Construction of the Zone of Proximal Development in Adult-Child Joint Action: The Socialization of Meals." In B. Rogoff and J. V. Wertsch (eds.), *Children's Learning in the "Zone of Proximal Development."* New Directions for Child Development, no. 23. San Francisco: Jossey-Bass, 1984.

Von Cranach, M., Doise, W., and Mugny, G. *Social Representations and the Social Bases of Knowledge.* Bern, Switzerland: Hogrefe and Huber, 1992.

Warton, P. M., and Goodnow, J. J. "Money and Children's Household Jobs: Parents' Views of Their Interconnections." *International Journal of Behavioral Development,* in press.

Wertheim, E. S. "The Science and Typology of Family Systems: Further Theoretical and Practical Considerations." *Family Processes,* 1975, *14,* 285–309.

JACQUELINE J. GOODNOW is professorial research fellow in the School of Behavioural Sciences, Macquarie University, Sydney, Australia.

The authors propose a model of change in parent-adolescent relationships involving recurring violations and realignment of interpersonal expectancies. Recent findings are consistent with this view of gradual dyadic adaptation to individual developmental change.

Parent and Adolescent Expectancies: Individual and Relational Significance

W. Andrew Collins, Coral Luebker

This chapter addresses the question of how changes in parent-adolescent relationships make it possible for parents to maintain continuity of significant functions in the socialization of their children. Changes in parent-child relationships have long been given a central role in theoretical accounts of adolescent development. Although altered interactions are considered fundamental to individual development (for example, Blos, 1979; Erikson, 1968; Freud, 1969), changes in parent-child relationships are typically characterized in negative terms of declining parental status and influence, increasing distance of children from parents, and decreasing positive emotional exchanges between them. Recently, however, the focus of theoretical and empirical work has shifted from the presumption of difficulties to examination of the nature and functions of parent-child relationships in development during adolescence (for example, Collins, 1990; Grotevant and Cooper, 1985; Hauser and others, 1984; Hill, 1988; Holmbeck and Hill, 1991; Paikoff and Brooks-Gunn, 1991; Smetana, 1988, 1989; Steinberg, 1987, 1988; Youniss and Smollar, 1985). This shift in focus emphasizes *continuity of function*—the continuation of relationships between parent and child that optimally support individual growth and development, appropriate to the developmental tasks faced by the child.

In the research discussed below, the premise is that continuity of function during adolescence, as in other periods, requires a dynamic balance between continuity and change in the nature and content of parent-child interactions.

This chapter is based on a paper presented at the biennial meeting of the Society for Research in Child Development, New Orleans, Mar. 1993.

Normatively, relationships with parents continue to be significant and positive forces in the development of most adolescents (Steinberg, 1990). Studies of ethnically and culturally diverse samples indicate generally positive views toward parents throughout adolescence, as well as substantial concordance between adolescents and their parents on such matters as vocational and educational decisions (DeSantis, Ketterlinus, and Youniss, 1990; Feldman and Quatman, 1988; Fuligni, 1991; Hill, 1988; Rutter, 1980). Furthermore, differences among families in emotional expression, openness to communication, provision of firm guidelines for behavior, and teaching orientation are correlated with differences in adolescent personality characteristics and behavioral patterns in much the same way that family and child differences are associated in earlier periods (Collins, 1990; Hill, 1988; Steinberg, 1990). These characteristics of interactions between parents and children have been found to be functional for healthy adolescent development, including identity formation, the development of social-cognitive skills, and ego development (Allen, Hauser, Bell, and O'Connor, 1994; Grotevant and Cooper, 1985; Hauser and others, 1984).

These continuities, however, occur within significant normative changes in the extent and particular forms of interaction that parents and children share. Parent-child interactions during late childhood and adolescence are marked by increased assertiveness by both parents and children (for example, Papini, Datan, McCluskey-Fawcett, 1988; Steinberg, 1981), increased incidence of conflicts (Montemayor, 1983; Montemayor and Hanson, 1985; Smetana, 1989; Steinberg, 1987), decreased expressions of physical affection and positive feelings among family members (Papini and Sebby, 1988; Papini, Roggman, and Anderson, 1991; Steinberg, 1988), and adjustments in the amount and kind of influence children exert in family decision making (for example, Jacob, 1974; Steinberg, 1981).

This coexistence of continuity and change has been characterized as a transformation in which emotional bonds are maintained, while interaction patterns are modified to make them more appropriate to the capabilities and orientations of maturing adolescents. Two key links between relationship transformations and individual development have been established. One is the link to adolescents' development of autonomy and achievement of a mature identity (Allen, Hauser, Bell, and O'Connor, 1994; Grotevant and Cooper, 1985, 1986; Steinberg, 1990). The other is the importance of this transformation process in the evolution of relationships within which parents and children continue to influence each other after childhood (Ainsworth, 1989; Frank, Pirsch, and Wright, 1990; Kobak and Sceery, 1988). These links are discussed throughout this chapter.

A Model of Expectancy Violation and Realignment in Relationships

Changes in the balance between continuity and change are consistent with an expectancy violation-realignment model of links between adolescent development and relationship change (Collins, in press). In this view, physical, social, and cognitive changes during the transition to adolescence give rise to frequent violations of the expectancies that mediate interactions in parent-child relationships, thus increasing the likelihood of perturbations in these interactions. These interactional difficulties in turn provide an impetus for both parents and children to form new age-appropriate expectancies, behaviors, and responses.

The expectancy violation-realignment model begins with the assumption that the interactions between parents and children are mediated by cognitive and emotional processes associated with expectancies about the behavior of other persons. In periods of rapid developmental change, such as the transition to adolescence, parents' expectancies are often violated. To maintain parent-adolescent relationships, and thus the opportunity for further influence on the adolescent's development, one or both parties often alter expectancies, behavior, or both to make expectancies more congruent. Repeated iterations of this process may occur over the course of adolescence in various behavioral domains.

Applying this key assumption to parent-adolescent relationships leads to two corollaries. One is that change in relationships is essential for adaptation to the rapid cognitive, socioemotional, and physical changes of the transition to adolescence. The second is that the primary mechanism of change involves violations of interpersonal expectancies, which stimulate parents and children to generate and coordinate new expectancies appropriate to the more symmetrical structures and coregulatory processes that characterize interactions between parents and their young adult offspring (Collins, 1990, in press).

This view of transformations links normal perturbations in parent-adolescent relationships to general processes of close relationships, that is, dyads typified by frequent, highly interdependent action sequences across diverse settings and tasks over a considerable period of time (Kelley and others, 1983). Interdependencies are natural products of parents' and children's shared histories and complementary roles. The expectancies that underlie ongoing parent-child relationships undoubtedly differ in content and complexity in different life periods, although little is known about the processes by which parents and children form different expectancies for each other in one period from those they held in earlier life periods.

Expectancy Violations and Parent-Adolescent Conflict

An implication of particular relevance to parent-adolescent relationships is that when expectancy violations occur, both interactional (for example, conflict) and emotional (for example, expression of negative affect and decreased satisfaction) perturbations can occur. Conflicts are normative events in relationships (Braiker and Kelley, 1979; Kelley and others, 1983; Montemayor, 1983; Shantz and Hartup, 1992). Mutual opposition or disagreement (Shantz, 1987; Vuchinich, 1987) arises naturally in connection with violations of expectations associated with age-graded transitions and maturational changes of the transition to adolescence. Although conflicts may be more frequently initiated and ineffectively managed in early adolescence, the involuntary (closed field) nature of parent-child relationships creates extra pressure for accommodation to altered capabilities and predilections of adolescents and to changes in relative power and autonomy within families.

Although the negative consequences of conflicts commonly are emphasized, whether conflicts are functional or dysfunctional depends on the characteristics of the relationships in which they occur (Collins and Laursen, 1992). Parent-adolescent relationships characterized by continuously high levels of conflict are associated with psychosocial problems during adolescence and in later life (Montemayor, 1983; Steinberg, 1990), whereas interactions that typically are marked by responsiveness to adolescents' expressions of discrepant opinions are associated with mature ego identity among the adolescents, as well as social perception and reasoning skills (Grotevant and Cooper, 1985, 1986; Walker and Taylor, 1991). Effectively managed conflict also fosters interpersonal adaptations necessitated by the physical, social, and cognitive changes of adolescence.

Previous research on parent-adolescent conflicts has been concerned primarily with documenting the topics associated with conflict, the frequency and intensity of occurrences, and, to a lesser extent, the relative frequencies of different types of resolutions (Collins and Laursen, 1992). Although a few studies have demonstrated correlations between the relative frequency and intensity of conflicts and stress in parents (Silverberg and Steinberg, 1990; Small, Eastman, and Cornelius, 1988) and in families (for example, Gehring, Wentzel, Feldman, and Munson, 1990), we are only now beginning to learn about the nature and processes of conflicts that arise in connection with normal developmental transitions during early adolescence and how these affect the satisfaction and well-being of parents and adolescents and the subsequent development of young persons.

Developmental issues in both generations may affect both the likelihood of expectancy violation and the process of forming or altering expectancies. For adolescents, these issues include the difficulty of integrating and coping with multiple intra- and extra-individual changes, as have been associated with constructs like identity (Erikson, 1968; Marcia, 1980).

Similar psychosocial issues have been attributed to the middle years of adulthood, the age of many parents of early adolescents (for example, Rossi, 1987). Coping with midlife personal, marital, and occupational stresses may affect parents' responses to the changes of adolescence and also parents' reactivity, emotional states, and levels of distraction from the tasks of parenting (for example, Aldous, 1978; Montemayor, McKenry, and Julian, 1993). Silverberg and Steinberg (1990) reported that when parents' orientation toward their paid work roles is weak, adolescent changes are often associated with a low sense of well-being; but when work orientation is strong, adolescent changes often are positively associated with well-being. Similarly, attitudes regarding marital relationships may be linked to relationships with offspring (for example, Montemayor, McKenry, and Julian, 1993).

Although difficulties in parent-adolescent relationships may be exacerbated by parental developmental issues and other stressors, a significant proximal context is expectancy violations by adolescents. Parent-child conflicts frequently occur in connection with adolescents' failures to meet expectancies regarding mundane responsibilities (for example, Montemayor, 1983; Steinberg, 1990). Beginning from this assumption, we have undertaken studies to address the hypothesis that the rapid changes of the transition into adolescence, whether from maturational or environmental sources, give rise to conflicts that stimulate parents and children to generate and coordinate new expectancies that are appropriate to the more symmetrical structures and coregulatory processes of parent-adolescent relationships (for example, Collins, 1990, in press; Hill and Holmbeck, 1986; Youniss and Smollar, 1985). This transition entails adaptations by both parents and adolescents.

We have established that such violations are particularly likely in early adolescence. At this age, both adolescents and their parents showed greater discrepancies between their perceptions of the other generation and their expectancies of ideal behavior of persons of those ages than did adolescents and parents in younger and in older groups (Collins, 1990, in press). Other studies also have documented similar age-related patterns with respect to disagreements between parents' and adolescents' views of jurisdiction over adolescents' behavior (Smetana, 1988, 1989) and in divergence in beliefs about adolescents' personal characteristics (Alessandri and Wozniak, 1987, 1989). These findings reflect cognitive development and broadening social knowledge among adolescents, as well as parents' age-graded expectations and prematurely stabilized beliefs about children's typical behaviors (Collins, 1990).

As an example of how violations of expectancies might occur, consider a preadolescent child who has typically been compliant and easy to manage but who begins more frequently to question, or seek rationales for, parents' demands. From the child's side, this behavior may reflect any one of a number of sources associated with early adolescent transitions. For example, the behavior might reflect experiences in other social settings such as the middle-school classroom or the peer group, where questioning and challenging are typical; or it may indicate partial, but not yet fully realized, concepts of reciprocity and mutuality in parent-child relations. Regardless, to the parents this behavior will probably seem resistant, even insolent, because it is a departure from the child's usual compliant behavior; and they may respond by applying extra pressure for compliance. For both the child and the parents, the violations of expected behavior and the negative exchanges and emotions that may follow them may result, over time, in modification of expectancies and behaviors toward one another. More positive examples are possible, as well, as when a child manifests incipient maturity earlier than parents had expected, or when adolescents are granted autonomy in some area even before they themselves begin to press for it because parents judge that they are "old enough." In terms of relationships, then, both positive and negative expectancy violations may stimulate *bilateral realignment* of expectancies that transform, but do not subvert, bonds between parents and adolescents (Collins, in press).

Relationship Change and Autonomy Transitions

The process of changes in close relationships is particularly significant for adolescent development when the convergence and divergence of expectancies are associated with the development of autonomy. Most theoretical formulations emphasize that individual changes associated with autonomy are significant to changes in parent-adolescent relationships. These views imply that parent-adolescent difficulties are particularly significant in connection with issues pertaining to psychosocial development (Blos, 1979; Hill and Holmbeck, 1986; Steinberg, 1990). Conflicts with parents have been considered integral to autonomy striving, and research findings document the covariation between the two (for example, Silverberg and Steinberg, 1990; Steinberg, 1987, 1988). For example, the most commonly reported conflict issues between parents and adolescents involve authority, autonomy, and responsibilities (Carlton-Ford and Collins, 1988; Montemayor, 1983; Smetana, 1989). Transitions associated with autonomy provide salient contexts within which to examine processes of change in parent-adolescent relationships.

Although most treatments of autonomy (for example, Blos, 1979) emphasize gaining freedom from parental regulation, autonomy is better understood as the acquisition of self-governance (Hill and Holmbeck, 1986). In parent-child relationships, autonomy involves gradually transferring regulation of adolescents' behaviors from parents to adolescents (Hill and Holmbeck, 1986). A period of coregulation (Maccoby, 1984; Smetana, in press) is typically involved in this transition in industrialized societies. Qualities of parent-child interaction significantly affect the impact of decision-making exchanges involved in coregulation; qualities of conflict resolution in family decision making have been linked to aspects of psychosocial development that underlie mature social interactions (for example, identity formation, the development of social-cognitive skills, and ego development) (Grotevant and Cooper, 1985; Hauser and others, 1984).

We have proposed (Collins and Luebker, 1991) that autonomy consists of multiple specific transitions to responsibilities over which parents have previously exercised jurisdiction. Parents' and adolescents' expectancies about the timing and significance of these transitions thus provide specific referents for examining both the nature of autonomy and adaptations to individual changes.

Autonomy and Conflict: New Findings

In our current studies, we are attempting to broaden the approach to parent-adolescent relationships in two ways, First, we are examining specific manifestations of behavioral transitions related to autonomy. To get at these transitions, we are assessing expectancies associated with transfers of responsibilities from parents to children, such as jurisdiction over clothing choices and school decisions. We are also examining transitions in activities over which parents typically exercise jurisdiction at earlier ages, but not later ones, such as whether to spend time with friends rather than family and use of tobacco or spirits. Second, our goal is to specify the expectancies associated with these transitions so that we can then examine explicitly their implications for relationships.

In our initial study, we examined expectancies about these transitions by conducting a timetable study. We asked both parents and adolescents to indicate the age they considered to be appropriate for forty-seven different transitions to occur before or during adolescence. Our questionnaire was completed by seventy-one mother-child pairs; fathers' responses were available in too few cases in this sample to permit reliable analyses. The families were grouped according to the age of the target adolescent: ten to twelve, thirteen to fifteen, and sixteen to seventeen years old.

We began by asking whether developmental transitions in different areas of responsibility or activity had already occurred. If the transition had occurred, we asked the age at which it occurred, and whether it was considered timely. If it had not occurred, we asked at what later age it would be appropriate. Parents and adolescents also completed two important ratings for each item: Adolescents were asked, "How important it is that you be able to do (the activity) at your age?" and parents were asked, "How important is it that your child *wait* to do this activity?" For all questions, we collected information from both parents and adolescents in order to examine the degree of *interpersonal* discrepancies in expectancies about adolescent behavior.

Our initial analyses focused on two questions:

To what degree are parents' and adolescents' expectancies about issues of adolescent autonomy likely to be violated? We found that discrepancies within the parent-adolescent dyads were very frequent indeed, both for responsibilities (such as choosing one's own clothes or hairstyle) and for activities (such as whether to date, smoke, or drink). Our data also showed little concordance between parents' and adolescents' expectancies regarding the appropriate time for specific transitions, implying that discrepancies are likely between both persons' expectancies and the behavior of the other.

What are the conditions under which these violations are most likely? The age of the child was important, with discrepancies generally more common—and violations thus more likely—in early adolescence. For example, we found that early-adolescent children were more likely to have engaged in activities and responsibilities without their mothers' recognition. Regardless of whether the thirteen- to fifteen-year-olds had made the transition to the more adultlike behavior, they, more so than the sixteen- and seventeen-year-olds, disagreed with their mothers about appropriate timing. Furthermore, mothers in both younger groups were more likely to place considerable importance on waiting to make the transition to more adultlike behavior, whereas thirteen- to fifteen-year-olds were as likely as sixteen- and seventeen-year-olds to rate adultlike activities as important to do.

With respect to discrepancies in judgments of appropriate timing, we found the fewest discrepancies in the oldest group, where a greater number of the adolescents were engaging in a wider variety of activities and responsibilities. This finding is contrary to some predictions in that opposition between the generations was tied not to the sheer number of "older" behaviors in which adolescents were engaging but rather to disagreements about timing. The finding is consistent, however, with our prediction that the views of parents and adolescents gradually converge as a result of successive iterations of realignments of expectancies, following violations. These cross-sectional data must be replicated longitudinally to provide the information that is needed to address this prediction.

In Search of Process in Relational Transitions

With these findings as a basis, our goal is to address two further questions. One of these concerns how change takes place. In our view, perceptions and expectancies of others' behaviors are significant to mechanisms whereby the multiple changes of adolescence—changes in biological, social, emotional, and cognitive domains—affect parent-child relationships during the transition to adolescence.

Our evidence that violations of expectancies are more likely during the transition to adolescence, however, leaves open the question of whether cognitive factors contribute to change. To address this question, we need to focus more broadly on aspects of cognition that may affect the expectancies that underlie parent-child interactions. For example, age-related changes may elicit different *attributions* about the causes of child behaviors from those parents have made at earlier points in development. Dix, Ruble, Grusec, and Nixon (1986) compared adults' responses to hypothetical misbehaviors by children and adolescents and found that the older the child, the more likely parents were to infer that the child understood that certain behaviors were wrong, that the transgression was intentional, and that the behavior indicated negative dispositions in the child. Furthermore, when parents inferred that the child was capable of self-control and that the misbehavior was intentional, they were more upset with the child, and they thought punishment, rather than discussion and explanation, was a more appropriate response. Clearly, transgressions by adolescents have a different significance from that of transgressions by younger children (Dix, Ruble, and Zambarano, 1989).

Expectancies and their interpersonal implications may also be affected by a variety of beliefs and assumptions about persons, relationships, and social roles. For example, parents' responses to violated expectancies are likely to be affected by whether the violation is relevant to their socialization goals or to an implicit developmental timetable (that is, whether the behavior is "off-time"). We are particularly interested in the conditions under which parents perceive violations as indications of relationship difficulties, as against those conditions under which they are simply considered as normative or as requiring corrective socialization, but without the imputation of threat either to the relationship or to the well-being of parent or child (Collins, 1992; Goodnow and Collins, 1990). For example, we predict that when perceived relationship-relevance is high, violations will lead to parent-child interactions marked by greater negative affect, communication difficulties, and reduced closeness (although conflict in the sense of disagreements and oppositions may be associated with both relationship-relevant and normative change violations). We also expect that in cases where discrepancy is evident even after the transition has occurred, interactions are more likely to include tension and conflict than when there is relative convergence in perceptions.

New findings from our research (Harris and Collins, 1994) provide clues to the conditions under which parents detect and respond to the relational implications of violated expectancies. In this work, we compared parents who differed in the degree of parent- versus child-centeredness and in the complexity of their conceptualizations of child development and parent-child relationships. We predicted that parents who held self-focused and conventional beliefs would react relatively more intensely to violations of socialization expectancies or personal preferences, whereas parents who were relatively more focused on other persons and the family system would react more intensely to violations of relationship expectancies. We termed the former group *categorical parents* and the latter group *perspectivistic parents.* We used Sameroff and Feil's (1985) measure of parental concepts of development with parents of children twelve to thirteen, fourteen to fifteen, and sixteen to seventeen years old, as well as interview measures of actual and hypothetical parent-adolescent conflicts. Our findings support our predictions, implying that general concepts of parent-child relationships may mediate reactions to violations of parental expectancies.

The second of our two questions that await further evidence concerns the extent to which violated expectancies press for a realignment of expectancies between adolescents and their parents. We have hypothesized that when previously congruent expectancies are violated by behavioral changes associated with adolescent development, parents and adolescents are stimulated to revise their expectancies of each other to make them more appropriate to the altered status of the child. We are now attempting to specify some of the conditions under which this continuous and fluctuating change process is especially likely to occur between parents and adolescents.

A key related question concerns the conditions under which parents detect and respond to violations. One possible approach to this question is based on the premise that reactions to perceived expectancy violations depend partly on the meaning assigned to the violations. Previous research indicates that the following six aspects of parents' cognitions about violations are especially relevant (Collins, 1992).

Parents' Goals. Violations that are perceived as threatening parental socialization goals are especially likely to elicit negative reactions from parents, and these reactions may be inimical to maintaining positive interactions. Parents should be asked to rate the importance or centrality of violations of behavioral expectancies to their goals as parents and to rate the relevance of specific behaviors to general principles that they have identified as significant socialization goals for them.

Implicit Developmental Timetables. Beliefs about the age at which specific competencies and psychosocial orientations should appear may engender inappropriate or unrealistic expectancies. Parents and other adults often hold well-differentiated expectancies about the course of development in the transition from childhood to adolescence and make specific inferences about the implications of these changes for individual functioning (for example, Collins, Schoenleber, and Westby, 1987; Hill and Lynch, 1983). Some studies (Feldman and Quatman, 1988; Rosenthal and Feldman, 1991) indicate that parental expectancies regarding autonomy transitions are similar across certain subcultural groups, but that discrepancies between parents' and adolescents' expectancies vary considerably across these same groups. Reaction to violations probably depends partly on the degree of differentiation in parents' ideas about the nature and course of development (Goodnow and Collins, 1990). Attainment of expected behaviors occurs at different times from one domain of competence and performance to another. The recognition of this diversity may enable parents to moderate reactions to violations, whereas the expectation of similar levels of maturity across domains may intensify negative reactions to violations. Similarly, the categorization of a discrepant behavior as largely a matter of personal preference, rather than of morality or conventionality, may make a perceived discrepancy less worthy of parental reaction (Smetana, 1988; Smetana and Asquith, 1994).

Attributions Regarding the Causes of Newly Appearing Behavioral Patterns. Parents are more likely to attribute perceived transgressions by adolescents, as opposed to those by children, to willfulness or disregard of behavioral standards (Dix, Ruble, and Zambarano, 1989). In married couples, attributions of negative interpersonal conditions to one's spouse have been found to be associated with subsequent reports of dissatisfaction with the relationship and with the incidence of conflicts (Fincham and Bradbury, 1987). Violated expectancies may similarly reduce positive feelings about the parent-child relationship, foster hostility and alienation, and otherwise impede positive interactions. In addition, parents who see themselves as having little power in dealing with unresponsive or resistant children have been found to have more highly negative emotional reactions and to engage in more peremptory behaviors toward children (Bugental and Shennum, 1984; Bugental, Blue, and Cruzcosa, 1989). Moreover, parents have reported lowest satisfaction with their parental roles when they perceive themselves as incapable of influencing a child's behavior on some characteristic that should, in principle, be open to influence and that other parents seem able to influence (Emmerich, 1969).

Inferences That the Violation Is Relevant to the Relationship. Several types of ideas may determine whether parents infer relationship difficulties from violations (Goodnow and Collins, 1990). One is the extent to which concern for relationships outweighs personal wants and needs. Studies of Italian families (New, 1988; Soccio, 1977) and black families in the rural United States (Heath, 1983) have documented how cultural values regarding concern for family over satisfaction of individual needs affect specific child rearing practices from infancy onward. For parents in such families, violations that imply self-concern rather than regard for the collective may elicit especially strong reactions. A second is the importance of reciprocity based on a communal, rather than an exchange, model (Clark, 1984). Expectancy violations that imply a perceived obligation to carry out certain actions or to behave in specific ways may elicit negative reactions because they are considered inappropriate to close, caring relationships. Conversely, parents who view the adolescent's failure to conform to expectancies as a failure to "repay" them for fulfilling their own role responsibilities may react to violations in ways that exacerbate relationship difficulties. A third is the degree to which boundaries among family members are respected and maintained. Perceived boundary transgressions may elicit especially strong reactions.

Extent to Which Parents Consider Repair of Relationships to Be a Requirement of the Parental Role. The impact of perceived relationship-relevant violations may be greatest when parents perceive that responsibility for rectifying the problem falls within the parental role. When parents do not consider this part of their responsibilities, violations may become a persistent obstacle to the kinds of relationships that foster positive psychosocial development during adolescence. Although little studied, a common speculation is that one aspect of dysfunctional parenting is the premature expectation that children bear responsibility for maintaining relationships with parents (for example, Emery, 1989; Parke and Collmer, 1975).

Particular Methods or Strategies That Are Believed to Be Necessary or Available to Parents in Attempting to Improve the Relationship. Responses to perceived relationship-relevant violations are likely to depend on ideas about how to reach agreement and resolve conflict (Goodnow, this volume; Goodnow and Collins, 1990). Limited information is available about adolescents' ideas, but parents' ideas about methods are likely to be affected by two general orientations (Goodnow and Collins, 1990). One is the degree to which consensus or joint decision making is viewed as a characteristic of "good" family relationships. Openness toward others' expressed opinions and respect for others' views may be the most important aspects of an apparent orientation to consensus. The second is the degree to which family members "should" make allowances for one another. These ideas imply a tolerance for behavioral variations that would portend a flexible, responsive family environment, with positive effects on offspring. In addition, they may buffer parents' own tendencies to react to violated expectancies in ways that might impair the quality of the parent-child relationship.

Conclusion

The view of parental cognitions invoked here is similar to other formulations that emphasize parents' beliefs and the convergence and divergence of parent and child scripts in child rearing (for example, Emmerich, 1969; Hess, 1981; Maccoby, 1984). We are simply extending these ideas to the particular issues raised by the rapid developmental changes of early adolescence and the importance of constructive parental responses in adolescents' psychosocial development.

It should be noted that cultural variations in interaction patterns within parent-adolescent relationships, in general, and in views about expectancy violations associated with autonomy, in particular, have been virtually unstudied (Jones, 1989; Taylor, Casten, and Flickinger, 1993); and few instruments and procedures have been properly developed for use with non-European American samples. The need for archival-quality data on these variations is great, especially as they pertain to groups that comprise large proportions of the U.S. population. Although little guidance exists for hypothesizing how parents and adolescents would manifest distinctive cultural orientations to the issues of interest here, several observations can be made on the basis of several key sources (Cooper, Baker, Polichar, and Welsh, 1993; Kelley, Power, and Wimbush, 1992; Phinney, 1990; Taylor, Casten, and Flickinger, 1993; Tolson and Wilson, 1990).

With respect to African American parents, for example, expectancy violations may be regarded less readily as having implications for relationships than is the case in European American families; rather, socialization concerns are likely to take precedence, partly because family concerns are assumed to transcend personal issues and because socialization responsibilities are viewed as more critical to the safety and success of African American youth (for example, Kelley, Power, and Wimbush, 1992). For similar reasons, African American parents and adolescents may expect a more limited range of possible resolutions to conflicts than do European Americans; research findings indicate a generally more authoritarian orientation, with greater expectation of unquestioning obedience, in African American families.

These recent findings are among our early steps toward new directions in our research on social-cognitive aspects of the parental role and parent-child relationships. These new directions emphasize that relationships develop in close association with individual changes in the transition to adolescence, with significant consequences for the subsequent development of the adolescent. We are attempting to examine one process by which these relational adaptations may occur and some developmentally significant conditions under which this process is most likely to come into play. We see parental cognitions about their children's behavior and the qualities of their relationships with them as a key element in understanding this process. Our eventual goal is to move from this element toward clear specification of the conditions under which changes in parent-adolescent relationships are likely to maintain the dynamic balance between continuity and change during the transitions of early adolescence.

References

Ainsworth, M.D.S. "Attachments Beyond Infancy." *American Psychologist,* 1989, *44*, 709–716.

Aldous, J. *Family Careers: Developmental Change in Families.* New York: Wiley, 1978.

Alessandri, S. M., and Wozniak, R. H. "The Child's Awareness of Parental Beliefs Concerning the Child: A Developmental Study." *Child Development,* 1987, *58,* 316–323.

Alessandri, S. M., and Wozniak, R. H. "Continuity and Change in Intrafamilial Agreement in Beliefs Concerning the Adolescent: A Follow-Up Study." *Child Development,* 1989, *60,* 335–339.

Allen, J. P., Hauser, S. T., Bell, K. L., and O'Connor, T. G. "Longitudinal Assessment of Autonomy and Relatedness in Adolescent-Family Interactions as Predictors of Adolescent Ego Development and Self-Esteem." *Child Development,* 1994, *65,* 179–194.

Blos, P. *The Adolescent Passage.* Madison, Conn.: International Universities Press, 1979.

Braiker, H. B., and Kelley, H. H. "Conflict in the Development of Close Relationships." In R. L. Burgess and T. L. Huston (eds.), *Social Exchange in Developing Relationships.* San Diego: Academic Press, 1979.

Bugental, D. B., Blue, J., and Cruzcosa, M. "Perceived Control Over Caregiving Outcomes: Implications for Child Abuse." *Developmental Psychology,* 1989, *24,* 532–539.

Bugental, D. B., and Shennum, W. A. *"Difficult" Children as Elicitors and Targets of Adult Communication Patterns: An Attributional-Behavioral Transactional Analysis.* Monographs of the Society for Research in Child Development, vol. 49, no. 1 (serial no. 205). Chicago: University of Chicago Press, 1984.

Carlton-Ford, S. L., and Collins, W. A. "Family Conflict: Dimensions, Differential Reporting, and Developmental Differences." Paper presented at the annual meeting of the American Sociological Association, Atlanta, Aug. 1988.

Clark, M. S. "Implications of Relationship Type for Understanding Compatibility." In W. Ickes (ed.), *Compatible and Incompatible Relationships.* New York: Springer-Verlag, 1984.

Collins, W. A. "Parent-Child Relationships in the Transition to Adolescence: Continuity and Change in Interaction, Affect, and Cognition." In R. Montemayor, G. R. Adams, and T. P. Gullotta (eds.), *Advances in Adolescent Development. Vol. 2: From Childhood to Adolescence: A Transitional Period?* Newbury Park, Calif.: Sage, 1990.

Collins, W. A. "Parents' Cognitions and Developmental Changes in Relationships During Adolescence." In I. E. Sigel, A. V. McGillicuddy-DeLisi, and J. J. Goodnow (eds.), *Parental Belief Systems: The Psychological Consequences for Children.* (2nd ed.) Hillsdale, N.J.: Erlbaum, 1992.

Collins, W. A. "Relationships and Development: Dyadic Adaptation to Individual Change." In S. Shulman and S. Strauss (eds.), *Relationships and Socioemotional Development.* Norwood, N.J.: Ablex, in press.

Collins, W. A., and Laursen, B. "Conflict and Relationships During Adolescence." In C. U. Shantz and W. W. Hartup (eds.), *Conflict in Child and Adolescent Development.* New York: Cambridge University Press, 1992.

Collins, W. A., and Luebker, C. "Change in Parent-Child Relationships: Bilateral Processes in the Transition to Adolescence." Paper presented at the biennial meeting of the International Society for the Study of Behavioral Development, Minneapolis, Minnesota, July 1991.

Collins, W. A., Schoenleber, K., and Westby, S. *The Behavior Expectancies Inventory: Middle-Class Adults' Expectancies for Eleven to Sixteen Year Olds.* Minneapolis: Institute of Child Development, University of Minnesota, 1987.

Cooper, C. R., Baker, H., Polichar, D., and Welsh, M. "Ethnic Perspectives on Values and Communication Among Adolescents and Their Fathers, Mothers, and Siblings." In S. Shulman and W. A. Collins (eds.), *Father-Adolescent Relationships*. New Directions for Child Development, no. 62. San Francisco: Jossey-Bass, 1993.

DeSantis, J., Ketterlinus, R., and Youniss, J. "Black Adolescents' Concerns That They Are Academically Able." *Merrill-Palmer Quarterly*, 1990, *36*, 287–299.

Dix, T. H., Ruble, D. N., Grusec, J., and Nixon, S. "Social Cognition in Parents: Inferential and Affective Reactions to Children of Three Age Levels." *Child Development*, 1986, *57*, 879–894.

Dix, T. H., Ruble, D. N., and Zambarano, R. J. "Mothers' Implicit Theories of Discipline: Child Effects, Parent Effects, and the Attribution Process." *Child Development*, 1989, *60*, 1373–1391.

Emery, R. E. "Family Violence." *American Psychologist*, 1989, *44*, 321–328.

Emmerich, W. *The Parental Role: A Cognitive-Functional Approach*. Monographs of the Society for Research in Child Development, vol. 34, no. 8. Chicago: University of Chicago Press, 1969.

Erikson, E. H. *Identity: Youth and Crisis*. New York: Norton, 1968.

Feldman, S. S., and Quatman, T. "Factors Influencing Age Expectations for Adolescent Autonomy: A Study of Early Adolescents and Parents." *Journal of Early Adolescence*, 1988, *8*, 325–343.

Fincham, F., and Bradbury, T. "The Impact of Attributions in Marriage: A Longitudinal Analysis." *Journal of Personality and Social Psychology*, 1987, *53* (3), 510–517.

Frank, S. J., Pirsch, L. A., and Wright, V. C. "Late Adolescents' Perceptions of Their Relationships with Their Parents: Relationships Among Deidealization, Autonomy, Relatedness, and Insecurity, and Implications for Late Adolescents' Adjustment and Ego Identity Status." *Journal of Youth and Adolescence*, 1990, *19*, 571–588.

Freud, A. "Adolescence as a Developmental Disturbance." In G. Caplan and S. Lebovici (eds.), *Adolescence: Psychological Perspectives*. New York: Basic Books, 1969.

Fuligni, A. J. "Parent-Adolescent Conflict in Japan, Taiwan, Hungary, and the United States." Paper presented at the biennial meeting of the International Society for the Study of Behavioral Development, Minneapolis, Minn., July 1991.

Gehring, T. M., Wentzel, K. R., Feldman, S. S., and Munson, J. "Conflict in Families of Adolescents: The Impact on Cohesion and Power Structures." *Journal of Family Psychology*, 1990, *3*, 290–309.

Goodnow, J. J., and Collins, W. A. *Development According to Parents: The Nature, Sources, and Consequences of Parents' Ideas*. Hillsdale, N.J.: Erlbaum, 1990.

Grotevant, H. D., and Cooper, C. R. "Patterns of Interaction in Family Relationships and the Development of Identity Formation in Adolescence." *Child Development*, 1985, *51*, 415–428.

Grotevant, H. D., and Cooper, C. R. "Individuation in Family Relationships: A Perspective on Individual Differences in the Development of Identity and Role-Taking in Adolescence." *Human Development*, 1986, *29*, 82–100.

Harris, M. L., and Collins, W. A. "Parental Perspective-Taking: Parental Correlates to Parent-Adolescent Conflict." Paper presented at the International Conference on Personal Relationships, Groningen, The Netherlands, July 1994.

Hauser, S. T., Powers, S. I., Noam, G. G., Jacobson, A. M., Weiss, B., and Follansbee, D. J. "Familial Contexts of Adolescent Ego Development." *Child Development*, 1984, *55*, 195–213.

Heath, S. B. *Ways With Words: Language, Life, and Work in Communities and Classrooms*. New York: Cambridge University Press, 1983.

Hess, R. D. "Approaches to the Measurement and Interpretation of Parent-Child Interaction." In R. W. Henderson (ed.), *Parent-Child Interaction: Theory, Research, and Prospects*. San Diego: Academic Press, 1981.

Hill, J. P. "Adapting to Menarche: Familial Control and Conflict." In M. R. Gunnar and

W. A. Collins (eds.), *Development During the Transition to Adolescence.* Minnesota Symposia on Child Psychology, vol. 21. Hillsdale, N.J.: Erlbaum, 1988.

Hill, J. P., and Holmbeck, G. N. "Attachment and Autonomy During Adolescence." *Annals of Child Development,* 1986, *3,* 145–189.

Hill, J. P., and Lynch, M. E. "The Intensification of Gender-Related Role Expectations During Early Adolescence." In J. Brooks-Gunn and A. C. Petersen (eds.), *Girls at Puberty.* New York: Plenum, 1983.

Holmbeck, G. N., and Hill, J. P. "Conflictive Engagement, Positive Affect, and Menarche in Families with Seventh-Grade Girls." *Child Development,* 1991, *62,* 1030–1048.

Jacob, T. "Patterns of Family Conflict and Dominance as a Function of Age and Social Class." *Developmental Psychology,* 1974, *10,* 1–12.

Jones, R. L. (ed.). *Black Adolescents.* Berkeley, Calif.: Cobb and Henry, 1989.

Kelley, H. H., Berscheid, E., Christensen, A., Harvey, J. H., Huston, T. L., Levinger, G., McClintock, E., Peplau, L. A., and Peterson, D. R. *Close Relationships.* New York: Freeman, 1983.

Kelley, M. L., Power, T. G., and Wimbush, D. D. "Determinants of Disciplinary Practices in Low-Income Black Mothers." *Child Development,* 1992, *63,* 573–582.

Kobak, R. R., and Sceery, A. "Attachment in Late Adolescence: Working Models, Affect Regulation, and Representations of Self and Others." *Child Development,* 1988, *59,* 135–146.

Maccoby, E. E. "Middle Childhood in the Context of the Family." In W. A. Collins (ed.), *Development During Middle Childhood: The Years from Six to Twelve.* Washington, D.C.: National Academy Press, 1984.

Marcia, J. E. "Identity in Adolescence." In J. Adelson (ed.), *Handbook of Adolescent Psychology.* New York: Wiley, 1980.

Montemayor, R. "Parents and Adolescents in Conflict: All Families Some of the Time and Some Families Most of the Time." *Journal of Early Adolescence,* 1983, *3,* 83–103.

Montemayor, R., and Hanson, E. "A Naturalistic View of Conflict Between Adolescents and Their Parents and Siblings." *Journal of Early Adolescence,* 1985, *5,* 23–30.

Montemayor, R., McKenry, P. C., and Julian, T. "Men in Midlife and the Quality of Father-Adolescent Communication." In S. Shulman and W. A. Collins (eds.), *Father-Adolescent Relationships.* New Directions for Child Development, no. 62. San Francisco: Jossey-Bass, 1993.

New, R. S. "Parental Goals and Italian Infant Care." In R. LeVine, P. M. Miller, and M. M. West (eds.), *Parental Behavior in Diverse Societies.* New Directions for Child Development, no. 40. San Francisco: Jossey-Bass, 1988.

Paikoff, R. L., and Brooks-Gunn, J. "Do Parent-Child Relationships Change During Puberty?" *Psychological Bulletin,* 1991, *110,* 47–66.

Papini, D. R., Datan, N., and McCluskey-Fawcett, K. A. "An Observational Study of Affective and Assertive Family Interactions During Adolescence." *Journal of Youth and Adolescence,* 1988, *17,* 477–492.

Papini, D. R., Roggman, L. A., and Anderson, J. "Early-Adolescent Perceptions of Attachment to Mother and Father: A Test of the Emotional-Distancing and Buffering Hypotheses." *Journal of Early Adolescence,* 1991, *11,* 258–275.

Papini, D. R., and Sebby, R. A. "Variations in Conflictual Family Issues by Adolescent Pubertal Status, Gender, and Family Member." *Journal of Early Adolescence,* 1988, *8,* 1–15.

Parke, R. D., and Collmer, C. "Child Abuse: An Interdisciplinary Analysis." In E. M. Hetherington (ed.), *Review of Child Development Research.* Vol. 5. Chicago: University of Chicago Press, 1975.

Phinney, J. "Ethnic Identity in Adolescents and Adults: Review of Research." *Psychological Bulletin,* 1990, *108,* 499–514.

Rosenthal, D. A., and Feldman, S. S. "The Influence of Perceived Family and Personal Factors on Self-Reported School Performance of Chinese and Western High School Students." *Journal of Research on Adolescence,* 1991, *1* (2), 135–154.

Rossi, A. "Parenthood in Transition: From Lineage to Child to Self-Orientation." In J. Lancaster, J. Altmann, A. Rossi, and L. Sherrod (eds.), *Parenting Across the Life Span: Biosocial Dimensions.* New York: Aldine de Gruyter, 1987.

Rutter, M. L. *Changing Youth in a Changing Society: Patterns of Adolescent Development and Disorder.* Cambridge, Mass.: Harvard University Press, 1980.

Sameroff, A. J., and Feil, L. A. "Parental Concepts of Development." In I. E. Sigel (ed.), *Parental Belief Systems: The Psychological Consequences for Children.* Hillsdale, N.J.: Erlbaum, 1985.

Shantz, C. U. "Conflicts Between Children." *Child Development,* 1987, *58,* 238–305.

Shantz, C. U., and Hartup, W. W. (eds.). *Conflict in Child and Adolescent Development.* New York: Cambridge University Press, 1992.

Silverberg, S. B., and Steinberg, L. "Psychological Well-Being of Parents with Early Adolescent Children." *Developmental Psychology,* 1990, *26,* 658–666.

Small, S. A., Eastman, G., and Cornelius, S. "Adolescent Autonomy and Parental Stress." *Journal of Youth and Adolescence,* 1988, *17* (5), 377–391.

Smetana, J. G. "Adolescents' and Parents' Conceptions of Parental Authority." *Child Development,* 1988, *59,* 321–335.

Smetana, J. G. "Adolescents' and Parents' Reasoning About Actual Family Conflict." *Child Development,* 1989, *60,* 1052–1067.

Smetana, J. G. "Context, Conflict, and Constraint in Adolescent-Parent Authority Relationships." In M. Killen and D. Hart (eds.), *Morality in Everyday Life: Developmental Perspectives.* New York: Cambridge University Press, in press.

Smetana, J. G., and Asquith, P. "Adolescents' and Parents' Conceptions of Parental Authority and Personal Autonomy." *Child Development,* 1994, *65,* 1143–1158.

Soccio, L. "A Family in Italy and Australia." In S. Murray-Smith (ed.), *Melbourne Studies of Education.* Melbourne, Australia: Melbourne University Press, 1977.

Steinberg, L. "Transformations in Family Relations at Puberty." *Developmental Psychology,* 1981, *17,* 833–840.

Steinberg, L. "Impact of Puberty on Family Relations: Effects of Pubertal Status and Pubertal Timing." *Developmental Psychology,* 1987, *23,* 451–460.

Steinberg, L. "Reciprocal Relation Between Parent-Child Distance and Pubertal Maturation." *Developmental Psychology,* 1988, *24,* 122–128.

Steinberg, L. "Interdependency in the Family: Autonomy, Conflict, and Harmony." In S. S. Feldman and G. R. Elliot (eds.), *At the Threshold: The Developing Adolescent.* Cambridge, Mass.: Harvard University Press, 1990.

Taylor, R. D., Casten, R., and Flickinger, S. M. "Influence of Kinship Social Support on the Parenting Experiences and Psychosocial Adjustment of African-American Adolescents." *Developmental Psychology,* 1993, *29,* 382–388.

Tolson, T.F.J., and Wilson, M. N. "The Impact of Two- and Three-Generational Black Family Structure on Perceived Family Climate." *Child Development,* 1990, *61,* 416–428.

Vuchinich, S. "Starting and Stopping Spontaneous Family Conflicts." *Journal of Marriage and the Family,* 1987, *49,* 591–601.

Walker, L., and Taylor, J. "Family Interactions and the Development of Moral Reasoning." *Child Development,* 1991, *62,* 264–283.

Youniss, J., and Smollar, J. *Adolescent Relations with Mothers, Fathers, and Friends.* Chicago: University of Chicago Press, 1985.

W. ANDREW COLLINS is professor in the Institute of Child Development, University of Minnesota, Minneapolis.

CORAL LUEBKER is a doctoral candidate in the Institute of Child Development.

Mothers across a wide range of cultures and social classes believe that in order for children to establish autonomy and personal identity, the children should have choice and decision-making power over some personal behaviors. Mothers' concepts about the personal domain of children have implications for theories of self and social values formation.

Mothers' Beliefs Regarding the Personal Domain of Children

Laurence Nucci

Despite the many controversies now energizing discourse on human development, there is convergence around the notion that, beginning at some point in infancy or childhood, all psychologically intact persons experience themselves as agents capable of decision making and the initiation of action (Crapanzano, 1990; Geertz, 1984; Stern, 1985). Recently, it has been proposed that in order to maintain agency and a differentiated personal identity, children require areas of behavioral choice or discretion in what has been referred to as the personal domain (Nucci and Lee, 1993; Nucci, in press).[1] While the personal is central to the child's establishment of self, the construction of what is private or personal is not an autochthonous achievement involving only the child's initiation of requests or claims to freedom of action. It is socially constructed out of negotiation and input from others (Nucci, in press; Nucci and Lee, 1993). The child's exercise of choice, however, often takes place in the context of relationships that are inherently asymmetrical. Since children are dependent on adult protection, nurturance, and teaching, a child's freedom of action is almost always at the mercy of adults. This is especially the case in relations between children and parents, where issues of adult authority and responsibility are intertwined with parental tendencies to invest their own familial and personal identities in their children. An interesting question, then, is how parents conceptualize their authority in relation to children and, specifically, whether parents view it as important for children to have a personal arena of behavioral choice. This chapter takes up that issue with regard to the beliefs of mothers.

Mothers' beliefs about how to interact with their children draw from several sources and reflect their own conceptions of children's psychological requirements, as well as more general cultural theories of child rearing and cultural notions of the role of the individual in relation to the family or larger social group. I take up the issue of cultural factors in relation to mothers' beliefs about the personal areas of children's lives in some detail later through discussion of studies that were conducted with mothers and children in Brazil. An important source of information that mothers within any culture use to construct their beliefs about children and mothering is their interactions with their own children. It is an axiom of constructivist theories of child development that children develop their social understandings out of their interactions with others. These interactions, however, do not supply information solely to the child; they also serve to convey information to others regarding the child's states, needs, and perspectives. One way to begin a discussion of mother's beliefs about children's social regulation is to look at patterns of social interaction between mothers and their young children. Such interactions provide evidence as to whether mothers provide children an area of behavioral discretion and also reveal features of children's behavior that mothers may draw from to supplement or alter their beliefs about children's requirements for areas of personal choice.

Mother-Child Interactions and the Personal Domain in Early Childhood

The one study that has looked at mother-child interactions around personal issues was conducted within the United States with twenty middle-class suburban mothers and their three- or four-year-old children (Nucci and Weber, in press). This particular sample was chosen because of the likelihood that the mothers would provide their children opportunities to exercise personal choice. The U.S. middle class has been described as an individualistic rights-based culture (Miller, Bersoff, and Harwood, 1990; Shweder, Mahapatra, and Miller, 1987), and thus Nucci and Weber (in press) viewed it as a context in which interactions pertaining to personal issues would likely take place between mothers and their preschool children. Moreover, authors such as Erikson (1950) and Gesell (1928), who have influenced American views of children, have argued that early childhood is critical for the establishment of children's autonomy and personal self-confidence. They have been joined by others who have counseled American mothers of the need to engage in forms of parenting that take a middle ground between constraint and permissiveness in order to foster positive social-emotional outcomes in children (Baumrind, 1988; Brazelton, 1989; Spock and Rothenberg, 1985). These general views of children, while encouraging mothers to be flexible, have not provided an empirical or theoretical account of just what sorts of things mothers ought to control and what they should allow children to decide for themselves (see Smetana, this volume, Chapter Two, for a detailed treatment of this issue).

Building on domain-theory-based research on social interactions in the home pertaining to moral and conventional issues (Smetana, 1989b), Nucci and Weber (in press) examined how interactions pertaining to personal matters differed from interactions regarding issues of interpersonal regulation. In addition, they looked at whether and in what ways interactions pertaining to personal issues differed from interactions pertaining to the class of actions that Tisak and Turiel (1984) termed *prudential*. Prudential issues refer to children's actions that result in, or have the potential to result in, harm to the children. Prudential actions are related to personal issues in that they pertain to the actor rather than to others. However, since such actions result in harm to the child, they fall within the scope of parental interests to foster the welfare of their own children (Smetana, 1989a; Tisak and Tisak, 1990). One would predict, then, that mothers will respond differently to such prudential actions in comparison to other actions in the child's personal sphere.

Mother-child dyads were observed during four activity periods over a span of three days. Trained coders classified transcribed event sequences as moral, conventional, prudential, personal, or mixed. These interaction sequences were then examined in two ways. First, the overall form of the interactions was classified as to whether the social messages directed at children contained explicit or indirect information about the social meaning of a given action, and whether the interaction resulted in negotiation involving some degree of concession by the mother. Second, the mothers' and children's individual statements and actions were assigned to behavioral categories. Analyses of the overall form of interactions indicated that the use of explicit social messages characterized 70 to 85 percent of events involving moral, conventional, or prudential events. In contrast, less than one-third of interactions about personal issues conveyed explicit social messages that the behavior in question was clearly within the child's authority.

An example of an interaction with an explicit social message is the following excerpt from a discussion between a mother and her daughter over the girl's hairstyle.

MOTHER: If you want, we can get your hair cut. *It's your choice.*
CHILD: I only want it that long—down to here. [Child points to where she wants her hair cut.]

More typically, the social messages that mothers directed to their children about personal issues were in the indirect form of offered choices, such as illustrated in the following exchange:

MOTHER: You need to decide what you want to wear to school today.
CHILD: [Opens a drawer.] Pants. Pants. Pants.
MOTHER: Have you decided what to wear today?
CHILD: I wear these.
MOTHER: Okay, that's a good choice. How would you like your hair today?
CHILD: Down. [Child stands by the bed, and her mother carefully combs her hair.]

In the second interaction, the mother, through a set of offered choices, conveys the idea that dress and hairstyle are matters for the child to decide. The child might accordingly infer that such behavior is personal. Through both the direct and indirect forms of communication, mothers evidence a willingness to provide children areas of personal discretion. The greater tendency for mothers to use direct messages in the context of moral, conventional, and prudential events than in the context of personal ones is in itself an indication that mothers view the former as issues in which the child needs to accommodate specific external social demands and meanings, whereas the personal issues are for the child to idiosyncratically interpret and control. This differential overall response pattern was carried through in the mothers' tendency to negotiate in response to children's resistance to the mothers' behavioral requests for a given social action.

Mothers almost never negotiated with children regarding moral, conventional, or prudential forms of conduct. On the other hand, nearly one-quarter of the observed interactions around personal issues involved negotiation and concession by the mothers. What is also interesting is the degree to which negotiations took place in the context of mixed events. Over 90 percent of the observed mixed events involved overlap with the personal domain. Mothers engaged in negotiation with their children in the context of such mixed events about half of the time. This type of interaction over a mixed issue is illustrated in the following:

MOTHER: Evan, it's your last day of nursery school. Why don't you wear your nursery sweatshirt?

CHILD: I don't want to wear that one.

MOTHER: This is the last day of nursery school, that's why we wear it. You want to wear that one?

CHILD: Another one.

MOTHER: Are you going to get it, or should I?

CHILD: I will. First I got to get a shirt.

MOTHER: [Goes to the child's dresser and starts picking out shirts.] This one? This one? Do you know which one you have in mind? Here, this is a new one.

CHILD: No, it's too big.

MOTHER: Oh, Evan, just wear one, and when you get home, you can pick whatever you want, and I won't even help you. [Child puts on shirt.]

This case presents a conflict between a dress convention (wearing a particular shirt on the last day of school) and the child's view that dress is a personal choice. The mother acknowledged the child's resistance and attempted to negotiate, finally offering the child a free choice once school was over. This example illustrates several things. The mother provided direct information to the child about the convention in question: "This is the last day of nursery school, that's why we wear it." At the same time, the mother exhibited an interest in fostering the child's autonomy and decision making around the issue. The child's resistance, which conveyed the child's personal interest, was not simply cut off but was guided by the mother, who linked it to the child's autonomy: "Are you going to get it, or should I?" "You can pick whatever you want, and I won't even help you." In the end, there is compromise. The child got to choose, but within a more general conventional demand (enforced by the mother) that he wear a shirt.

The verbal dance of the mother-child dyad in the above example is further illustration that the mothers in this study acted in ways that indicated an understanding that children should have areas of discretion and personal control. The excerpt also illustrates ways in which the children, through their resistance, provided mothers with information about the child's desires and needs for personal choice. Analyses of the individual responses of the children indicated that assertions of prerogative and personal choice did not occur to the same degree across all forms of social interaction but instead were disproportionately associated with events involving personal issues. Assertions of prerogative and choice comprised 88 percent of children's responses in the context of mixed events, and 98 percent of their responses in the case of predominantly personal events. In contrast, such responses comprised less than 10 percent of children's statements in the context of moral or prudential events, and about 25 percent of their responses to conventional events. These behavioral measures indicate that middle-class, preschool-age children have differentiated conceptions of the personal from matters of interpersonal social regulation. Interviews conducted with the children revealed that they viewed personal, but not moral or conventional, behaviors as matters that should be up to the self and not the mother to decide.

Nucci and Weber's (in press) observational study provides evidence that middle-class mothers act in ways indicative of a conceptual differentiation between children's areas of personal choice and matters of moral and social regulation and prudence. Mothers displayed a systematic differences in their responses to their children as a function of whether the issues in question were within the children's personal domain. The study also provides evidence that children play an active role in relation to their mothers, and that they provide feedback in the dual form of requests and resistance to their mothers that affords mothers information regarding the children's claims to areas of personal control. This feedback is not simply a generalized resistance to adult authority (Brehm and Brehm, 1981; Kuczynski, Kochanska, Radke-Yarrow, and Girnius Brown, 1987) but a delimited set of claims to choice over a personal sphere. This set of claims is most evident in cases of mixed events and suggests that mothers open to their children's feedback have direct access to information about their own children's needs for a personal domain. Smetana's (1989a) work on adolescent-parent conflicts indicates that similar types of child resistance to adult control over what children view as personal continues throughout development as children move away from status as dependents and subordinants to status as adults (Youniss and Smollar, 1985).

Mothers' Beliefs About the Personal Domain of Children

In addition to the observational evidence of mothers' acknowledgment of children's areas of personal choice, mothers' views of these issues have been directly obtained through interviews. Two basic techniques have been employed. The first asks mothers to respond to standardized stimulus items depicting actions from the moral, conventional, prudential, and personal categories. The second employs open-ended interviews in which mothers are asked to articulate their views of whether or not children should be given decision making or choice in some areas of activity. In a recent study employing the first interview procedure, Nucci and Smetana (1994) examined the beliefs of forty mothers with children either four or six years of age. The social class of the mothers ranged from working to upper-middle class with annual family incomes from $10,000 to in excess of $100,000. The interview involved a sorting task in which mothers were presented sets of hypothetical scenarios depicting children engaged in actions that exemplified transgressions of moral (hitting and hurting, stealing) or conventional norms (standing while eating at the dinner table), or prudential (safety) concerns (not wearing warm clothing on a cold day, engaging in dangerous play). Mothers were also presented items depicting children engaged in actions that fit the definition of the personal (for example, picking out what color sweater to wear, deciding on a particular form of safe play or recreation) along with issues that were multifaceted or mixed, in which prudential or conventional concerns overlapped with personal ones. Items were presented in a standardized random order, and for each item mothers were asked to indicate whether the act was one the mother should control was up to the child, or was negotiable and could go either way.

Mothers' responses demonstrated that they viewed issues of morality, social convention, and prudence as under mothers' control. On the other hand, only a small handful of the mothers felt that issues of friendship choice, completely finishing all food, form of fantasy play, or choice of sweater to wear were things that mothers should decide. Instead, three-fourths of the mothers felt that these personal matters should be left up to the child. Issues that were viewed as negotiable tended to be issues that the majority of mothers had identified as within the child's area of choice, or they were mixed issues, such as playing with a "rough" child, that contained elements of personal choice. In sum, the mothers' treatment of these hypothetical items closely matched the actual behavior of the mothers described in the Nucci and Weber (in press) observational study.

Using a similar sorting task, Smetana and Asquith (1994) obtained essentially the same results in interviews with middle-class parents of children between the ages of eleven and eighteen. In their study, parents were asked to indicate which items were legitimately subject to parental control. As was the case with parents of young children, these parents viewed moral, prudential, and conventional issues as legitimately subject to parental control. Personal issues, however, were judged by parents as issues that should not be subject to their control. Parents were more equivocal in their judgments of multifaceted issues entailing overlap with the personal. With age, however, parents tended to see these issues as less legitimately controlled by parents and coming under adolescents' jurisdiction.

The pattern of responses to standardized stimulus items confirmed that mothers differentiate between their areas of legitimate control and areas that should be left up to children. These findings from sorting task procedures have been fleshed out by mothers' responses to open-ended interviews. These studies have focused on the beliefs of mothers of young children. The first of these was conducted with preschool-age children as a part of the Nucci and Weber (in press) observational study. An even more detailed picture of mothers' beliefs about these issues was provided in a follow-up study (Nucci and Smetana, 1994) of mothers with children four or six years of age. The interview consisted of a series of open-ended questions that addressed such issues as (1) whether there were things that children ought to decide and what those things would be and why, (2) what things parents ought to decide and why, (3) whether children should be permitted to hold their own opinions about things and why, (4) what the mothers saw as their own role in cases where they disagreed with the child's decision, (5) whether and around what sorts of issues parents and children should negotiate, and (6) whether people are individuals, and, if so, at what point a child becomes an individual and how. All of the mothers in both studies stated that children three to six years of age should be permitted to make decisions about certain issues and should be permitted to hold personal opinions about things. In terms of what sorts of things children should be allowed to decide for themselves, the mothers spontaneously listed clothing, food type and amount, friends or playmates, and other issues the mothers simply referred to as "inconsequential." The criteria mothers used to determine whether an issue should be left up to the child included concerns for safety, whether it contributed to the child's competence, was developmentally appropriate, was a matter of the child's personal domain, and conformed to the mother's general parental experience. In addition, all of the mothers in the Nucci and Smetana (1994) study responded affirmatively to the question of whether it was important for a child to develop a sense of individuality. They expressed a desire for their children to establish uniqueness, autonomy, competence, and agency. They saw their own role in this process as that of nurturer and educator. Few mothers defined their maternal role as that of controller or playmate. Finally, these mothers expressed the view that individuality emerges in infancy as an intrinsic human feature, or in toddlerhood with the advent of language.

The middle-class American mothers in these interview studies displayed a set of beliefs about children's areas of personal control that is concordant with theoretical differentiation between the personal and other forms of social conduct. Mothers did not present a uniform controlling or permissive orientation to their children but instead were controlling with respect to those aspects of children's behavior that fell within the purview of parental guidance and responsibility, and permissive with respect to those areas that fell within the children's personal domain. Actions or issues of substantial overlap with the children's personal area formed the social terrain around which mothers professed to negotiate with their children. Finally, mothers presented a developmental orientation in which criteria such as a child's competence and social status (adolescent versus child) were associated with an expansion of the child's personal area to include issues of personal safety and some issues of overlap with familial convention (Smetana and Asquith, 1994). The mothers' orientation toward children's areas of personal control reflected a set of underlying beliefs about the role that the personal plays in the development of children. These mothers expressed the belief that an area of personal discretion is necessary for children to develop agency, self-esteem, competence, autonomy, and personal identity. In other words, mothers attributed functional importance to their decisions to allow and even to foster an area of personal control in their children.

The beliefs presented by mothers in these interview studies are also concordant with the views expressed by children in studies of children's conceptions of parental authority (Smetana, 1988; Smetana, 1993; Smetana and Asquith, 1994; Tisak, 1986; Tisak and Tisak, 1990). Those studies indicate that children view it as legitimate for parents to establish rules governing children's moral, conventional, and prudential behaviors. Moreover, children hold that parents have an obligation to establish rules about moral issues (Smetana and Asquith, 1994). In addition, children maintain that parents should have broader authority over younger children than they should over adolescents (Smetana and Asquith, 1994; Tisak and Tisak, 1990). Indeed, it is discrepancies between what children and parents view as matters of the child's personal discretion that form the basis of most issues of adolescent-parent conflict (Smetana, 1989a).

The observed correspondence between the views of mothers and children may be attributable to a set of underlying developmental dynamics to which the parties are responding. On the other hand, this correspondence may simply reflect a set of powerful cultural beliefs in the individual being played out among members of the American middle-class household. Since what is considered personal varies to some degree from one culture to another, it is possible that mothers' beliefs about the function or even the existence of the personal in children might be culturally variable. This is a complex and difficult question to answer. Research that has examined views of parental authority and the personal outside of the U.S. middle class is, however, beginning to shed light on this issue. We turn now to that research.

Culture and Class Effects on Mothers' Beliefs About the Personal

Culture and Conceptions of Parental Authority. Research on parental authority has historically tended to frame the issue as a question of degree along a single dimension. For example, the most influential system for looking at parental tendencies to control children's actions is Baumrind's (1971) division of parenting types into the categories *permissive, authoritative,* and *authoritarian,* in which permissive and authoritarian represent the polar extremes of parental control. Applications of this unidimensional typology to members of social class and cultural groups that differ from the U.S. white middle class have, however, proved to be riddled with bias and misunderstanding. The cultural significance of parental behaviors labeled by the typology as authoritarian is not captured within the global, unidimensional framework of the typology. Baumrind (1972) was among the first to caution against simplistic applications of her typology. In a study examining the child rearing practices of African American parents, Baumrind discovered that parental actions that fit within the authoritarian pattern within white families did not result in an authoritarian "syndrome" among African American girls. Instead, the apparently authoritarian parental practices fostered toughness and self-sufficiency in the girls and were perceived by the daughters as "nurturant care-taking" (Baumrind, 1972, p. 266). In line with Baumrind's interpretation, Bartz and Levine (1978) found that African Americans, relative to whites, expected children to overcome childhood dependencies as soon as possible. This held true with education level controlled. African Americans and whites in the Bartz and Levine (1978) study did not differ, however, in their tendencies to emphasize children's general rights and their right to have input into family decisions.

The mismatch between white American views of parental authoritarianism and views of parenting in other cultures was perhaps best captured by Chao (1993), who argued that depictions of parental behaviors as authoritarian, controlling, and restrictive are typically ethnocentric and misleading. Asian families, for example, have been found to obtain among the highest scores of unquestioning obedience to parents on the Baumrind measure. To label such tendencies as authoritarian, according to Chao, is to misread behaviors that are based on Confucian conceptions of respect for elders. According to Chao, parental concern and love are equated in Asian cultures with firm control and governance. In related research, Rohner and Pettengill (1985) reported that Korean children's perceptions of parental warmth tend to increase as overall parental control increases. According to Rohner and Pettengill, this reflects a more general cultural view of the individual as a "fractional part" of the family. Consequently, decisions that are usually considered to be individual matters in white, middle-class families the United States are often the subject of scrutiny and approval in Korean families.

Just as it is an error to apply a unidimensional American conception of parental authority to others, it is an oversimplification to accept unidimensional descriptions of parental authority generated by members of other cultures as descriptive of themselves. In a study of Chinese adolescents, Lau and Ping (1987), for example, found that the positive relation between parental control and children's self-esteem and perceptions of parental warmth held only for parental behaviors that served organizational needs and not simply parental efforts to dominate or restrict the child. According to Lau and Ping, it is important to distinguish organizational from dominance or power-assertive forms of control. Jung and Turiel (1994) found that Korean children do not hold an uncritical view of parental authority but instead evaluate authority in terms of their independent judgments of the act and the context. For example, Korean children were found to reject the legitimacy of a parental command to commit harm. Similarly, Yau and Smetana (1994) reported that Chinese adolescent-parent relations were not without conflict (although less so than in the United States), and that conflicts were over the same types of issues as found with their American counterparts. Most interesting for our purposes here is that the adolescents in their study positioned their arguments in terms of exercising personal jurisdiction.

In sum, cross-cultural studies of parental authority provide a complex picture that mitigates against the assignment of simple global labels such as authoritarian or permissive, and individualistic or collectivistic, to the parenting practices of cultures or groups. Parenting practices that appear on the surface to be authoritarian or permissive from the perspective of an outsider may have a very different meaning to members within a cultural group. In addition, there is little evidence that the parenting practices of the majority of members of a culture fit within any single typology. As the Lau and Ping (1987) research on Chinese families demonstrated, there are variations in parental behavior even within what, on the surface, appears to be a single dimension of restrictive parenting. Moreover, the Yau and Smetana (1994) findings argue against simplistic views of parent-child relations as harmonious or conflict-free within so-called collectivistic societies (Baumrind, 1973). Given the complex picture of parenting and parent-child relations provided by the extant research, it is clear that caution needs to be exercised in any effort to extend research about mothers' beliefs about children's areas of personal choice to members of non-Western cultures. In taking these cultural factors into account, however, it is important to resist tendencies to view cultures as homogeneous and to assume that personhood and the individual are concepts of concern only to what are referred to as individualistic cultures. With these cautionary thoughts in mind, I turn now to research that has directly investigated culture and class effects on mothers' beliefs about the personal in children.

Brazilian Mothers' Beliefs About the Personal Domain of Children. Nucci, Camino, and Sapiro (1993) examined the impact of social class on mothers' views of children's areas of personal choice through interviews with lower- and middle-class mothers from two regions of Brazil. Brazil was thought to be a good context to study mothers' views of these issues for two reasons. First, Brazil, particularly its northeastern region, has been characterized as a collectivistic culture in comparison with the United States (Triandis and others, 1988). Second, researchers employing the Baumrind typology have characterized the parenting of Latino groups in the United States as authoritarian (Bartz and Levine, 1978; Laosa, 1980). With regard to this second point, it is worth noting that Laosa (1980) found that the authoritarian pattern held only for members of the lower economic class. Nucci, Camino, and Sapiro (1993) interviewed a total of 120 mothers. One-half of the sample lived in the large industrial city of Pôrto Alegre in southern Brazil. Pôrto Alegre is culturally similar in many respects with the United States and Europe. The population of the city is European in origin, and the middle and upper-middle classes are well off by Brazilian standards. The second half of the sample was from the northeastern coastal city of Natal. As noted before, the northeastern region of Brazil is considered less individualistic than the United States or Western Europe (Triandis and others, 1988). In addition, the region as whole is less affluent than southern Brazil. About 70 percent of families earn $60 per month or less and are considered members of the lower class. One-half of the mothers in Nucci, Camino, and Sapiro's (1993) study were from the lower class as defined by family income, and one-half were from the middle and professional classes as defined by family income and father's occupation. Twenty of the mothers from each region had an eldest child six to eight years of age, twenty had a child ten to twelve years of age, and twenty had a child fourteen to sixteen years of age.

The interviews used the same procedure as was employed in the Nucci and Smetana (1994) study of American mothers of young children. The first portion of the interviews with Brazilian mothers consisted of open-ended questions used by Nucci and Smetana (1994), which elicited mothers' views about children's autonomy and parental authority. Each mother was asked to respond to these questions in terms of a child the same age as her own oldest (target) child. The second part of the interview asked the mothers to respond to a set of standardized descriptions of children's behaviors. The issues used in the study were selected by Brazilian researchers as ones that fit within the theoretical definitions of the moral, conventional, personal, and prudential categories. Mothers were asked to indicate for each item whether it was an action that the mother should control, should be up to the child, or was negotiable and could go either way.

The general pattern of the Brazilian mothers' responses to the second, sorting task procedure was in line with responses obtained with U.S. samples. Brazilian mothers from both regions of the country and from both social classes tended to treat personal items as matters that should be up to the children, and compliance with moral and conventional norms as matters that the mother should not simply leave up to the child. Thus, the Brazilian mothers, like their U.S. counterparts, acknowledged an area of personal behavioral choice for their children. The Brazilian findings, however, also revealed regional and class differences within these broad overall trends. Mothers from southern Brazil and middle-class mothers from both regions were less likely to classify items as up to the parent and more likely to treat items as negotiable than were mothers from northeastern Brazil and lower-class mothers from both regions. That is, the northeastern and lower-class mothers seemed somewhat more authoritarian than the southern and middle-class mothers.

Results from the open-ended interviews helped to flesh out these responses. When asked whether there were some things that children of ages similar to their own should be allowed to make decisions about, the majority of lower-class mothers of adolescents and middle-class mothers of children and adolescents from both regions of Brazil responded affirmatively. This affirmative response was similar to that provided by the U.S. mothers of young children in the Nucci and Smetana (1994) study. The majority of lower-class mothers of six- to eight-year-old children from both regions of Brazil, however, responded in the opposite direction. When asked to give reasons for their responses, lower-class Brazilian mothers of young children gave prudential (risks to the child) and pragmatic reasons. That is, they felt that it would be either too dangerous or impractical to give young children decision-making authority over their actions. In contrast, like U.S. mothers of young children, Brazilian middle-class mothers of children and adolescents and Brazilian lower-class mothers of adolescents gave reasons supporting their children's emerging autonomy, agency, and personal competence. Similarly, the majority of lower-class mothers of six- to eight-year-old children did not think that parents should allow a child as old as theirs to have his or her own opinion about things, while a majority of all other mothers felt that children were entitled to opinions of their own. In the view of the lower-class mothers of young children, their youngsters had not matured sufficiently to have the reasoning capacity to form opinions.

Brazilian mothers who responded affirmatively to the proposition that children should have choice about some things spontaneously listed activities or issues similar to those listed by U.S. mothers. As reported by Smetana and Asquith (1994), the number of items left up to the child increased as a function of child age to include issues that mothers had previously viewed as matters of prudence (safety). In adolescence, mothers extended the child's personal areas of choice to include academic and occupational decisions as well as extended the adolescent's range of motion (where the child is permitted to be without seeking parental permission) and control over personal time. The criteria mothers used to decide whether an issue should be left up to the child were the same across regions and social classes. These criteria included concerns for the child's safety and whether the issue contributed to the child's competence, was developmentally appropriate, and was a matter of the child's private or personal domain.

It is noteworthy that Brazilian mothers from all of the groups, including lower-class mothers of young children, responded affirmatively to the question of whether it was important for a child to develop a sense of individuality. Indeed, language referring to individual autonomy was spontaneously employed during the interviews by the Brazilian mothers irrespective of region or class. They regarded fostering individuality in their children as important for establishing uniqueness, autonomy, competence, and agency. That is, the Brazilian mothers expressed essentially the same concerns in this regard as did the U.S. sample in the Nucci and Smetana (1994) study. Finally, Brazilian mothers were asked to indicate at what age they believed individuality developed. There were class differences in response to this question. Lower-class Brazilian mothers tended to place the age of individuality at adolescence (when "reasoning" emerges), while middle-class Brazilian mothers placed the onset of individuality at infancy or toddlerhood.

Nucci, Camino, and Sapiro's (1993) study with Brazilian mothers demonstrates that beliefs about children's personal choice are not confined to mothers from individualistic cultures. Across social classes and geographical regions, the Brazilian mothers expressed beliefs that children require areas of choice for their personal growth. The manner in which these beliefs were expressed, however, varied as a function of the mothers' underlying assumptions about the nature of their children's needs and capacities. Middle-class mothers, particularly from the southern "modern" region of the country, held views of young children essentially like those of mothers of the U.S. middle class. According to their view, children are to be treated as individuals from infancy and given opportunities to exercise choice to enhance their individual talents and personalities. That middle-class view was at variance with the perspective of the more traditional lower-class mothers, who viewed the limited cognitive capacity of infants and young children as an indication that they were not yet to be considered individuals with choice or opinions of their own. Nonetheless, even these traditional mothers valued the eventual emergence of individuality and agency in adolescence and distinguished the adolescent's rights to personal behavioral control from those moral or conventional zones of behavior that are the shared responsibility of parents and others.

Conclusion

The research reviewed in this chapter provides evidence that mothers from diverse cultural backgrounds tend to believe that children should be provided some behavioral choice in order to foster their individuality, autonomy, and personal competence. The age at which children are given control over their own actions and the range of actions children are permitted to treat as matters of individual choice vary both as a function of social class and culture and as a function of particular family circumstances. It does not appear, however, that provision of choice to children is limited to Western culture; rather, this allowance seems to be a ubiquitous feature of mother-child relations. This is particularly the case with respect to interactions with children in late childhood and adolescence. Mothers typically do not hold to a generalized disposition toward any and all forms of behavior but instead tend to limit the child's areas of discretion to actions that conform to theoretical definitions of the personal (Nucci, 1977). In contrast to their apparent permissiveness with respect to the child's personal areas of action, mothers believe that they should control or direct the child's actions toward desired forms of conduct with respect to issues of morality and social convention, along with control of actions that threaten the child's safety or health. Thus, it appears that mothers have a differentiated view of their responsibilities with respect to their children's actions that reflects mothers' beliefs about children's requirements for psychological and social development.

Mothers' beliefs about the emergence of the personal in their own children raise a set of interesting issues for theories of child development and socialization. Culture and class variations in the beliefs that mothers hold are evidence that socially constructed assumptions about the nature of children and the social meaning of children's actions are important components in the formation of such maternal beliefs. The role and meaning of adult authority vary considerably across class and cultural lines. In addition, assumptions about the nature and needs of children, such as whether to use physical punishment (Wainryb, 1993) or when a child can be expected to employ rational decision making, which stem from a storehouse of cultural folk wisdom, affect how an individual mother interprets a child's actions and how she should effectively respond. These undeniably collective constructions about children are not, however, all that seems to be operating in mothers' construction of beliefs about the personal choice requirements of their children. As was evidenced in observational studies of mother-child interactions (Nucci and Weber, in press) and in research on adolescent-parent conflict (Smetana, 1989a; Yau and Smetana, 1994), children provide direct input into their parents' constructions of such beliefs through their resistance to parental authority and claims to personal choice. Such resistance and claims by children are not confined to members of contemporary or Western culture but also appear as a feature of growing up in collectivist cultures (Yau and Smetana, 1994).

Commonalities in mothers' beliefs about children's needs for personal choice are, perhaps, most parsimoniously explained as corresponding to a set of underlying fundamental characteristics of children that emerge regardless of cultural setting. In particular, individual mothers and generations of mothers (as expressed through cultural schemes) are responding to children's psychological requirements for agency and personal identity that form the essential features of selfhood (Damon and Hart, 1988). While "self"-like beliefs about the personal are culturally variable, all cultures contain some differentiated view of self, and members of all cultures appear to hold idiosyncratic individualistic views of themselves as distinct persons with particular interests (Spiro, 1993). Mothers' beliefs about the needs of their children appear to take into account these psychological requirements for the formation of individuality, agency, and autonomy. Through their interactions with children around issues of personal choice and control, mothers help to situate their children's idiosyncratic constructions of selves in a particular cultural and temporal space.

Note

1. In that account, the personal is differentiated from the moral and the social-conventional regulation of interpersonal conduct. The personal refers to the set of actions that pertain only to the actor and that are, therefore, considered by the actor to be outside of justifiable

social regulation. These actions make up the private aspects of one's life and are subject not to considerations of right and wrong but rather to preferences and choice (Nucci, 1977, 1981; Smetana, 1982). Examples of personal issues within North American culture include the content of one's diary and self-expressive creative works, one's choice of friends or intimate associates, and actions that focus on the state of one's own body (Nucci, 1981; Nucci and Herman, 1982; Nucci, Guerra, and Lee, 1991; Smetana, 1982). Although the specific content of the personal is influenced by cultural norms (Miller and Bersoff, 1992), identification of a personal set of actions is thought to manifest broader core requirements for establishing personal boundaries for the self as object and related requirements (for personal agency, continuity, and uniqueness) for establishing a sense of self as subject (Nucci, in press). Thus, it has been proposed that individuals within all cultures seek to establish areas of personal choice in response to this set of fundamental psychological requirements.

References

Bartz, K. W., and Levine, E. S. "Child Rearing by Black Parents: A Description and Comparison to Anglo and Chicano Parents." *Journal of Marriage and the Family,* 1978, *40,* 709–719.

Baumrind, D. "Current Patterns of Parental Authority." *Developmental Psychology Monographs,* 1971, *4* (1, pt. 2).

Baumrind, D. "An Exploratory Study of Socialization Effects on Black Children: Some Black-White Comparisons." *Child Development,* 1972, *43* (1), 261–267.

Baumrind, D. "The Development of Instrumental Competence Through Socialization." In A. D. Pick (ed.), *Minnesota Symposia on Child Psychology,* vol. 7. Minneapolis: University of Minnesota Press, 1973.

Baumrind, D. "Rearing Competent Children." In W. Damon (ed.), *Child Development Today and Tomorrow.* San Francisco: Jossey-Bass, 1988.

Brazelton, T. B. *Toddlers and Parents.* New York: Delacorte Press/Lawrence, 1989.

Brehm, S. S., and Brehm, J. W. *Psychological Reaction: A Theory of Freedom and Control.* San Diego: Academic Press, 1981.

Chao, R. K. "Clarification of the Authoritarian Parenting Style and Parental Control: Cultural Concepts of Chinese Child Rearing." Paper presented at the 60th biennial meeting of the Society for Research in Child Development, New Orleans, Mar. 1993.

Crapanzano, V. "On Self-Characterization." In J. W. Stigler, R. A. Shweder, and G. Herdt (eds.), *Cultural Psychology: Essays on Comparative Human Development.* New York: Cambridge University Press, 1990.

Damon, W., and Hart, W. *Self-Understanding in Childhood and Adolescence.* New York: Cambridge University Press, 1988.

Erikson, E. H. *Childhood and Society.* New York: Norton, 1950.

Geertz, C. " 'From the Native's Point of View': On the Nature of Anthropological Understanding." In R. A. Shweder and R. LeVine (eds.), *Culture Theory: Essays on Mind, Self, and Emotion.* New York: Cambridge University Press, 1984.

Gesell, A. *Infancy and Human Growth.* New York: Macmillan, 1928.

Jung, M. K., and Turiel, E. "Korean Children's Concepts of Adult and Peer Authority." Unpublished manuscript, Graduate School of Education, University of California, Berkeley, 1994.

Kuczynski, L., Kochanska, G., Radke-Yarrow, M., and Girnius Brown, O. "A Developmental Interpretation of Young Children's Non-Compliance." *Developmental Psychology,* 1987, *23* (6), 799–806.

Laosa, L. M. "Maternal Teaching Strategies in Chicano and Anglo-American Families: The Influence of Culture and Education on Maternal Behavior." *Child Development,* 1980, *51* (3), 759–765.

Lau, S., and Ping, C. C. "Relations Between Chinese Adolescents' Perceptions of Parental

Control and Organization and Their Perception of Parental Warmth." *Developmental Psychology*, 1987, 23 (5), 726–729.

Miller, J. G., and Bersoff, D. M. "Culture and Moral Judgment: How Are Conflicts Between Justice and Interpersonal Responsibility Resolved?" *Journal of Personality and Social Psychology*, 1992, 62, 541–554.

Miller, J. G., Bersoff, D. M., and Harwood, R. L. "Perceptions of Social Responsibilities in India and the U.S.: Moral Imperatives or Personal Decisions?" *Journal of Personality and Social Psychology*, 1990, 58, 33–47.

Nucci, L. P. "Social Development: Personal, Conventional, and Moral Concepts." Unpublished doctoral dissertation, Psychology Board of Studies, University of California, Santa Cruz, 1977.

Nucci, L. P. "The Development of Personal Concepts: A Domain Distinct from Moral or Societal Concepts." *Child Development*, 1981, 52 (1), 114–121.

Nucci, L. P. "Morality and Personal Freedom." In T. Brown, E. Turiel, and E. Reed (eds.), *Knowledge and Values*. Hillsdale, N.J.: Erlbaum, in press.

Nucci, L. P., Camino, C., and Sapiro, C. M. "Mothers' and Children's Concepts of Areas of Children's Personal Autonomy and Social Regulation in the United States and Brazil." Paper presented at the 12th biennial meeting of the International Society for the Study of Behavioral Development, Recife, Brazil, July 1993.

Nucci, L. P., Guerra, N., and Lee, J. Y. "Adolescent Judgments of the Personal, Prudential, and Normative Aspects of Drug Usage." *Developmental Psychology*, 1991, 27 (5), 841–848.

Nucci, L. P., and Herman, S. "Behavioral Disordered Children's Conceptions of Moral, Conventional, and Personal Issues." *Journal of Abnormal Child Psychology*, 1982, 10 (3), 411–426.

Nucci, L. P., and Lee, J. Y. "Morality and Personal Autonomy." In G. G. Noam and T. Wren (eds.), *The Moral Self: Building a Better Paradigm*. Cambridge, Mass.: MIT Press, 1993.

Nucci, L. P., and Smetana, J. G. "Mothers' Conceptions of Young Children's Personal Domain." Unpublished manuscript, College of Education, University of Illinois at Chicago, 1994.

Nucci, L. P., and Weber, E. K. "Social Interactions in the Home and the Development of Young Children's Conceptions of the Personal." *Child Development*, in press.

Rohner, R. P., and Pettengill, S. M. "Perceived Parental Acceptance and Rejection and Parental Control Among Korean Adolescents." *Child Development*, 1985, 566 (3), 524–528.

Shweder, R. A., Mahapatra, M., and Miller, J. G. "Culture and Moral Development." In J. Kagan and S. Lamb (eds.), *The Emergence of Morality in Young Children*. Chicago: University of Chicago Press, 1987.

Smetana, J. G. *Concepts of Self and Morality: Women's Reasoning About Abortion*. New York: Prager, 1982.

Smetana, J. G. "Adolescents' and Parents' Conceptions of Parental Authority." *Child Development*, 1988, 59 (2), 321–335.

Smetana, J. G. "Adolescents' and Parents' Reasoning About Actual Family Conflict." *Child Development*, 1989a, 60 (5), 1052–1067.

Smetana, J. G. "Toddlers' Social Interactions in the Context of Moral and Conventional Transgressions in the Home." *Developmental Psychology*, 1989b, 25 (4), 499–508.

Smetana, J. G. "Conceptions of Parental Authority in Divorced and Married Mothers and Their Adolescents." *Journal of Research on Adolescence*, 1993, 3 (1), 19–39.

Smetana, J. G., and Asquith, P. "Adolescents' and Parents' Conceptions of Parental Authority and Adolescent Autonomy." *Child Development*, 1994, 65 (3), 1143–1158.

Spiro, M. "Is the Western Conception of the Self 'Peculiar' Within the Context of the World's Cultures?" *Ethos*, 1993, 21, 107–153.

Spock, B., and Rothenberg, M. B. *Dr. Spock's Baby and Child Care*. New York: Pocket Books, 1985.

Stern, D. *The Interpersonal World of the Infant: A View From Psychoanalysis and Developmental Psychology.* New York: Basic Books, 1985.

Tisak, M. "Children's Conceptions of Parental Authority." *Child Development,* 1986, 57 (1), 166–176.

Tisak, M., and Tisak, J. "Children's Conceptions of Parental Authority, Friendship, and Sibling Relations." *Merrill-Palmer Quarterly,* 1990, 3, 347–367.

Tisak, M., and Turiel, E. "Children's Conceptions of Moral and Prudential Rules." *Child Development,* 1984, 55 (3), 1030–1039.

Triandis, H., Bontempo, R., Villareal, M., Asai, M., and Lucca, N. "Individualism and Collectivism: Cross-Cultural Perspectives on Self-Ingroup Relationships." *Journal of Personality and Social Psychology,* 1988, 59, 1006–1020.

Yau, J., and Smetana, J. G. "Adolescent-Parent Conflict Among Chinese Adolescents in Hong Kong." Unpublished manuscript, University of Hong Kong, 1994.

Youniss, J., and Smollar, J. *Adolescent Relations with Mothers, Fathers, and Friends.* Chicago: University of Chicago Press, 1985.

Wainryb, C. "The Application of Moral Judgments to Other Cultures: Relativism and Universality." *Child Development,* 1993, 64 (3), 924–933.

LAURENCE NUCCI is professor of educational psychology in the College of Education at the University of Illinois at Chicago.

INDEX

ORDERING INFORMATION

NEW DIRECTIONS FOR CHILD DEVELOPMENT is a series of paperback books that presents the latest research findings on all aspects of children's psychological development, including their cognitive, social, moral, and emotional growth. Books in the series are published quarterly in Fall, Winter, Spring, and Summer and are available for purchase by subscription and individually.

SUBSCRIPTIONS for 1994 cost $54.00 for individuals (a savings of 25 percent over single-copy prices) and $75.00 for institutions, agencies, and libraries. Please do not send institutional checks for personal subscriptions. Standing orders are accepted.

SINGLE COPIES cost $17.95 when payment accompanies order. (California, New Jersey, New York, and Washington, D.C., residents please include appropriate sales tax.) All orders will be charged postage and handling.

DISCOUNTS FOR QUANTITY ORDERS are available. Please write to the address below for information.

ALL ORDERS must include either the name of an individual or an official purchase order number. Please submit your order as follows:
    Subscriptions: specify series and year subscription is to begin
    Single copies: include individual title code (such as CD59)

MAIL ALL ORDERS TO:
    Jossey-Bass Publishers
    350 Sansome Street
    San Francisco, California 94104-1342

FOR SUBSCRIPTION SALES OUTSIDE OF THE UNITED STATES, contact any international subscription agency or Jossey-Bass directly.